BEST
Breakfast Eats
IN
MISSOURI

Ann M. Hazelwood

REEDY PRESS
St. Louis, Missouri

Reedy Press
PO Box 5131
St. Louis, MO 63139

Library of Congress Control Number: 2011933010

ISBN: 978-1-935806-05-9

Please visit our website at www.reedypress.com.

Design by Alvin Zamudio

Printed in the United States of America
11 12 13 14 15   5 4 3 2 1

CONTENTS

ACKNOWLEDGMENTS

Many folks were nice enough to accompany me on my breakfast journeys. Eating breakfast alone rarely happened in my travels, as the day's first meal is very social, and the breakfast workers and owners were more than happy to join in on the conversation.

My husband, Keith Hazelwood, was a trooper on some visits, but since his hours are precious as an attorney, I did not succeed in taking him to as many restaurants as I would have liked. My son, Joel Watkins, happens to love breakfast, so when his busy schedule allowed, he didn't mind Mother picking up the tab for breakfast! My friends Terry David, Dellene Olendorff, Bobbie Kuschel, and Terry Gulickson were great breakfast companions. I was blessed with having a sister-in-law, Mary Hazelwood, and brother-in-law, John Hazelwood, who were hungry and agreeable.

Thanks to my husband's law firm, Hazelwood and Weber, I had the pleasure of signing my books at the Missouri Mayor's Conference when they visited St. Charles. I was fortunate and thankful to be able to ask many of those folks where their favorite breakfast spots were in their communities. If you shared breakfast with me in any of these spots, thanks for being there and adding your two cents. I'll be back!

INTRODUCTION

As some folks say, "It's 7:00 a.m. somewhere." Good morning, good day, or good night! Breakfast is permissible at all times of the day and night. Breakfast is personal. We can control what it will be like when we order it or how we make it. Breakfast is a compound word of "break" and "fast." We are breaking the fast from the last meal.

Health experts claim the breakfast we eat at the start of our day is the most important meal of the day. It often includes a carbohydrate such as cereal, fruit, protein, and sometimes a dairy product, and coffee, juice and hot tea are the typical drinks of choice.

A good thing to know about eating breakfast is that it may help to control your weight, according to Mayo Clinic nutritionist Katherine Zeratsky, RD. Breakfast helps reduce hunger later in the day and keeps us from overeating. Prolonged fasting when skipping breakfast can increase your body's insulin response, which in turn increases fat storage and weight gain.

Breakfast foods tend to be healthier choices. They are usually more nutritious and lower in fat, if fried options are avoided. Eating breakfast gives us energy, increasing our activity throughout the day. It refuels and replenishes the glycogen stores that supply blood sugar. Dr. Mark Pereira of the Harvard Medical School says you are less likely to develop diabetes if you eat breakfast.

Breakfast will vary around the world. A Japanese breakfast is based on rice, seafood, and fermented foods. Green tea is the choice of a breakfast beverage. In Denmark it's all about the bread and cereals served with tea or coffee. England has a heartier cooked breakfast that includes items such as eggs, sausage, bacon, black pudding, fried bread, mushrooms, and tomatoes. France, Italy, and Belgium are known for what we call a continental breakfast. Germany and Austria love bread rolls with jam. They will have cold cuts, cheeses, and a soft-boiled egg if they are really hungry. Tea, coffee, and orange juice are common beverages served. Cuba's urban areas serve café con leche, which is sweetened. Toasted Cuban bread cut into lengths is perfect for dunking in coffee. The Irish eat fried eggs, bacon rashers, sausages, white pudding, black pudding, sautéed potatoes, and tomatoes, topped with bacon soda bread and very strong tea.

Our breakfast in America is as American as apple pie. We value our farmland and the farmers who offer fresh meat, dairy, vegetables, fruit, and eggs that provide great breakfast food. They are now more accessible than ever to the average consumer through the many farmers' markets around the state. Many of them wholesale to commercial markets, which makes them available any time of the year. Much of Missouri is rural, and folks have been raised with healthy breakfasts. A good breakfast with a great cup of coffee has certainly been an American tradition.

Restaurants who serve breakfast all day are crowd pleasers, to say the least. It's comforting to know there are early risers preparing foods to start our day. Many chefs, cooks, bottle washers, and waitresses work tirelessly for little money to make sure this meal is timely and delicious. A big greeting, smile, tip, and thank you can certainly make their day.

After writing *100 Unique Eats and Eateries in Missouri*, I realized how much people loved sharing their food and eating experiences. They read the book, put it in the car, and traveled the Missouri regions, sampling my recommendations of eateries. Many asked the owners and chefs to sign their page, thus recording their visit and making it more personal. Their feedback has, in turn, helped me to explore more food destinations around the state. My conversations with them told me they were ready for more. I was more than ready to do so and knew they wanted to know more about breakfast establishments. Breakfast places have gone unnoticed and under appreciated by meal critics and authors. I knew more and more people were choosing to eat their first meal out of the house. Preparing breakfast can take time, which they do not have, and it can create a messy kitchen, which they do not need at the start of their day.

Note that I am not a food critic; however, I know from my experiences as a writer and breakfast consumer what I should look for to give you the best breakfast experience. Diners, neighborhood restaurants, tea rooms, and even a few bed-and-breakfasts were chosen to give you a sampling of the variety in our state.

Bonuses in this book are breakfast hints, tips, and quotes to enhance the topic. Perhaps I was having too much fun writing this book, but a steady diet of buttered, fluffy pancakes with crazy toppings might give you a breakfast buzz as well! I look forward to hearing from you on which breakfast spots gave you a buzz!

EATERIES, DINERS, AND DIVES

When a restaurant acquires a reputation as a great breakfast spot, it has a lot to live up to. These places can easily be found in any community by simply asking, "Hey, where can you get a good breakfast around here?" The local folks rarely hesitate with their answer. Their faces light up as they cheerfully tell you about their favorite breakfast place and in the same breath mention the food item they fondly remember.

In smaller places—like eateries, diners, and dives—the food is the centerpiece. We like the place to be clean but overlook many things when the food is plentiful and delicious and our appetite is satisfied. Here are ten things you can expect from such a quality dining establishment:

1. *The breakfast should be quick and timely. It is the first meal of the day in most cases. Our job and other activities are awaiting.*

2. *We expect the food to be homemade, which can be a broad term meaning:*

    a. no pancakes from a mix.

    b. preserves as well as apple-butter

    c. fresh fruit, not canned

    d. real oatmeal

    e. corn beef hash served their way

    f. over-easy eggs with yolk intact

    g. biscuits and gravy made that day

    h. freshly baked breads and muffins

3. *Breakfast eaters should be able to express how they want*

their breakfast served. They will tell how they want their eggs cooked and how crispy their bacon should be. It is critical to most to have their coffee strong and hot. Their breakfast has an "all about me" component.

4. *Regulars usually order the same menu item over and over, so they expect the same size, portion, or sides to be consistent every day. It tends to be what is most popular in that particular restaurant.*

5. *Reasonable prices: Customers want to come often, and with affordable prices, they can!*

6. *The dress code should be casual, meaning patrons can come in their workout or work clothes.*

7. *They usually have counters with stools, or a place where someone can sit alone and enjoy breakfast. This is enhanced by usually sitting where others are close by having breakfast, in case they want to visit.*

8. *Most folks just like the basics of a breakfast menu. Restaurants can give them clever names, but the ingredients used should be listed clearly. This is not the place to try gourmet recipes.*

9. *Folks expect large proportions. Customers will remember the amount served more than the taste in many cases. They plan on overeating and feeling uncomfortable and full when they leave. An establishment should be prepared to offer paper containers for leftovers.*

10. *Patrons like a family atmosphere. It should and can be "where everyone knows your name" kind of place. People expect to meet the owner or cook, and can feel comfortable bringing children or even an outspoken uncle and not be embarrassed.*

BRUNCHES

A brunch is a portmanteau (a kind of suitcase) of breakfast and lunch. Typically after 10:00 or 11:00 a.m., a brunch is advertised as a fancier way of eating a heavier meal to satisfy you until dinner is served.

Most brunches provide a buffet of many entrées of breakfast and lunch food items. This gives customers their choice of what they might be ready to eat that particular time of day. Some restaurants offer menu items, which is good to know when planning your visit.

Brunches tend to be offered in fine dining establishments or hotel restaurants that typically do not offer a breakfast menu. They can also be found in ethnic places that also may not offer a breakfast menu. Brunches are usually more expensive than a typical breakfast. The variety and number of dishes, combined with more expensive foods like shrimp, are understandably the reason for higher prices.

The clientele is generally in dress/casual attire or more formal dress because of the more upscale atmosphere. Brunches do not have "take home" options, unlike typical breakfast establishments. People have a tendency to generously load up more on their plate than they can possibly eat, and will likely go back for more.

Chefs that create your food options for a brunch are very conscious of presentation. It gives them an opportunity to compete with other chefs, not only in the presentations but the uniqueness of the foods and their taste. In finer restaurants, ice sculptures and other decorations accentuate the presentation. Ice sculpture competitions often feature well-known chefs.

Participants at a brunch have a leisurely approach to

their meal. They take more time to enjoy each course or dish and then return to try more. With this opportunity of so many choices, one is likely to try things strange to their palette. Their level of trust is there with the chef and restaurant. Studies show that most people choose the breakfast options on the brunch table over the lunch options. Perhaps this is because it is the first meal of the day for most. Sometimes there are servers behind the brunch buffet, and other buffets are self-serving. Cooks are usually there to prepare a fresh omelet, waffle, or a slice of ham or beef.

WHAT MIGHT BE OFFERED AT A BRUNCH?

- *the freshest fruit of the day*
- *hand-squeezed orange juice*
- *a variety of meats including freshly sliced ham and beef*
- *scrambled eggs or made-to-order eggs benedict*
- *oatmeal made from scratch with many toppings of choice*
- *assorted seafood and shrimp*
- *soufflés and potato offerings*
- *pastries from elaborate scones to bagels*
- *fresh salads*
- *desserts to die for; cakes, pies, bread pudding, tarts, cookies, and ice cream*
- *healthy choices are available for the asking, like sugar-free syrup and egg whites*
- *cocktails are permissible for brunch like the popular "Bloody Mary"*

Brunches seem to attract attention for celebrating special occasions like anniversaries and birthdays, because it allows all parties to be in a festive environment, and yet have their own choices of food. Reservations would be advised for such an event. Sundays and special holidays seem to be common brunch times. The after-church crowd often takes advantage of a brunch experience.

BED-AND-BREAKFASTS (B&Bs)

We have many choices when we travel today. Staying at a bed-and-breakfast can add a special and more personal touch to a trip by offering additional atmosphere and delicious food for breakfast. Your B&B hostess knows the competition is steep among their peers, so she wants to make your stay an unforgettable experience. The breakfast menus are usually gourmet compared to our home-cooked meals. Many try to use their family or original recipes. The fresh pastries and oven dishes emit aromas that will fill the breakfast table in a timely fashion. Rest assured, if your stay is more than one night, they will have a different menu the next morning.

When making your reservation, be sure to tell them your diet restrictions and food likes and dislikes, because they aim to accommodate. Hot meat and egg dishes and soufflés are very common on the B&B menus because they can be prepared the night before and popped in the oven the next morning. Pastries can vary greatly, but they are usually baked that morning, or perhaps choices will be offered by a local bakery. Local honey and preserves are bonuses. Most chefs at B&Bs brag about the locally grown products being used. Some have gardens in their back yard that contain herbs and fresh produce. Healthy choices are easily made at a bed-and-breakfast because of the knowledge of your diet. Hot coffee and juices are usually ready to serve before breakfast.

You may share your breakfast with other guests, and there is usually a choice of table options, so sharing a table is not required. Many find it interesting to converse about their travels.

A great bed and a good night's sleep make for a great visit, but waking up to a great breakfast is truly delightful!

BREAKFAST ON THE GO!

Up, go, and eat can easily be the routine of most busy folks these days! Breakfast is a big word, and we associate it with a block of time to feed our face the first thing in the morning. We know how difficult this can be when we would rather have a few more moments of sleep. Some do not consider a breakfast as we know it, except on the weekends.

If we had a penny for every meal we eat in our car, we would be rich. Our society multi-tasks all day long, so eating while driving is not uncommon to accomplish in our daily routine. Watching the line of cars go quickly through the drive-through at Starbucks, for example, is a good sign of how eager we are at this early hour. People are stressed and are looking for a quick kick to get them started on their day. Coffee choices continue to get stronger as well, and complicated blends are requested to keep us going longer.

Fast-food places like McDonald's know how to go heavy on their breakfast staff to keep the drive-through lines moving in a timely fashion. Most food choices can be handled with your hands while you hope the hot coffee remains inside the cup. If your coffee is brought from home, you will likely grab a breakfast bar or fruit as you go out the door. Most feel the "up, go, and eat" is permissible and no big deal because breakfast is the easiest meal to travel with and even skip. Children are sent to school with little or no breakfast, which affects their attitude and performance. Some schools offer a free breakfast for early arrivers because it adds such value to their day. A person's metabolism needs to be activated to start the day so calories can be consumed.

Some get their first cup of coffee when they arrive at work. This relaxed short frame of time gives us a moment to plan or think through our day or even visit with co-workers. Taking a "breakfast moment" to plan your day is a good thing. Whether you take the extra time to eat at home or visit one of the recommended breakfast stops, you will have a healthier start to your day, so now get UP, GO, AND EAT!

BEST
Breakfast Eats
IN
MISSOURI

DESSERT FOR BREAKFAST

Judy Howell and Sherry Pfaender, the owners of **Miss Aimee B's Tea Room and the Upstairs Marketplace**, did not lose sight of the past when they purchased the historic home of Aimee Marie Louise Becker. Visitors enter the restaurant through the backyard garden to the back porch and into the lavish hallway with its Victorian staircase.

The menu for this tea room is just as lavish and grand. The Peach Bomb dessert is popular for breakfast, so you may want to start with this seasonal choice. It's a whole peach wrapped in pie crust, baked, and then drizzled with almond butter.

For a heartier breakfast course, the Perfect Duo is just the thing. Divine Praline French Toast is served

A PERSONAL NOTE:
In their Cook Book II, the Dutch Baby Oven Pancake recipe explains the importance of a really hot skillet to make the best pancake. They suggest you heat the skillet at least fifteen minutes in a 425-degree oven before adding your butter.

with scrambled eggs embellished with paper-thin bacon that says life is good. The Dutch Baby Oven Pancake is a unique experience. It's a drop soufflé baked in a hot skillet and served with warm fruit. Yummy lunches abound as well. Special dinners are offered through the holidays.

You shouldn't leave until you visit the marketplace on the second floor. Five rooms contain crafts, fashion, and art that are anxious to go home with you. Don't forget to check out their cookbooks, which include many of their menu items, including the Peach Bomb. The tea room is located close to the historic district in St. Charles, so you can make a day of it. You will feel the spirit of Miss Aimee B. (literally) and will definitely want to return.

> "A WOMAN IS LIKE A TEABAG. IT'S ONLY WHEN SHE'S IN HOT WATER THAT YOU REALIZE HOW STRONG SHE IS."
>
> —Nancy Reagan

CONTACT INFO:
837 First Capitol Dr.
St. Charles
636-946-4202
missaimeeb.com

Breakfast served all day!

CHECK NUMBER NO. 3605140

ALL IS GOLDEN

When you fly into Lambert–St. Louis International Airport, look for the large sign advertising **The Golden Pancake**, which is across the street from the terminal. This spacious restaurant, once a Big Boy and Shoney's, has many large booths to seat the customers. Ahmad Khaf, the owner of four years, is proud of the extensive menu, which includes eight omelet choices and thirteen hearty breakfast combinations that can all be served with turkey bacon, turkey sausage, and turkey ham. Sizzling skillets are choices you see on many tables. There are four different combinations, served sizzling hot, and accompanied with toast.

The Golden Pancakes, however, are the center of attention, especially with the name that precedes it. The eight-inch pancakes are made totally from scratch with eggs, flour, and rich buttermilk. You can order three of these pancakes or homemade waffles; many request them with whipped cream and strawberries. It is a sight to behold for anyone's appetite. Children are extra pleased when they receive their Happy Face Chocolate Pancakes.

Ahmad makes sure he attends farmers' markets to get the freshest meats and produce. Healthy choices of cinnamon oatmeal and Egg Beaters are also available.

A PERSONAL NOTE:

Ahmad says to use only the freshest buttermilk for the pancakes. Always remember that the less you freeze anything, the better it will be.

This vintage-looking pancake house will take you back in time, and the food will not disappoint.

CONTACT INFO:

10216 Natural Bridge Rd.

St. Louis

314-427-0420

goldenpancake.com

Breakfast served all day!

A BREAKFAST SCENE

In the historic town of Hermann, the **Rivertown Restaurant** has formed its history since 1987. Joey and Mike Mirth, the current owners, feel that offering BIG portions has been one of the keys to their success.

The menu features many delightful choices, but the BIG favorite is the BIG Daddy's Breakfast. It offers an eleven-ounce chicken-fried steak, which is one of their signature meats, two eggs, hash browns, and two biscuits with gravy. The Breakfast Meal Deal Sandwich— one egg, one meat, with cheese grilled on your choice of bread—is also a big bargain. It comes with a side of biscuits, gravy, and hash browns for just $3.49.

A PERSONAL NOTE:

A welcome surprise when you visit the restaurant is viewing the ten original framed photos of the working riverboats going back to the 1800s. Many locals and relatives have memories they share when they come in to view the photos. These photos have been passed on through previous owners.

Joey tries to make sure he can utilize fresh Missouri produce for the ninety folks who can fill the tables and booths on busy days. The riverboat-themed restaurant is the perfect setting in this historic town, which was a German settlement dating back to 1837.

Visiting Hermann and having a BIG breakfast will be a BIG deal you'll remember.

"BREAKFAST IS A NOTORIOUSLY DIFFICULT MEAL TO SERVE WITH A FLOURISH."

— Clement Freud

Guest Check

CONTACT INFO:

CHECK NUMBER
N° 3605140

222 E. First St.
Hermann
573-486-4455
hermannhill.com/rivertown.htm

Breakfast served all day!

A TOTAL SOULARD EXPERIENCE

The Soulard Historic District in St. Louis is known for its festivities like Mardi Gras and Bastille Day. The famous and expansive Soulard Market is quite the regional attraction in itself. Businesses like the **Soulard Coffee Garden and Café** also offer a great experience and a good breakfast.

Owners Ted and Rita West have turned the Soulard Coffee Garden and Café into a true family enterprise. Ted and Rita now work shorter hours, but their son James and daughter Julie have picked up the slack and continue forward.

Their extensive menu encompasses omelets, like the Pappy, which combines smoked turkey, tomatoes, and guacamole topped with lemony hollandaise and tarragon. Breakfast sandwiches, eggs benedict choices, French toast, biscuits and gravy, eggs and hash browns, and the ever-popular Slinger are all available for the hungry customers. Many of these choices are known for being the "morning after" orders. Healthy choices like the fruit bowl, toast, and eggs are always available. You can build your own favorites by picking low-fat cheeses and vegetables. With the fresh produce market just blocks away from the café, you can

A PERSONAL NOTE:

The café offers a dense pancake made with cornmeal and served with fresh blueberries. It makes for a heartier meal and is served with real maple syrup.

be assured they will be using the freshest ingredients every day.

Catering services and room rentals for those special meetings and occasions are available as well.

"TELL ME WHAT YOU EAT, AND I WILL TELL YOU WHO YOU ARE."

—Jean Anthelme Brillat-Savarin

Guest Check

CONTACT INFO:

910 Geyer Ave.

St. Louis

314-241-1464

thecoffeegarden.food.officelive.com

Breakfast served all day!

CHECK NUMBER

N9 3605140

A FAMILY AFFAIR

A culinary visit to **Pumpernickles Delicatessen** in St. Louis introduces you to generations of loyal customers who appreciate good, traditional Jewish cooking.

When you enter the first of three rooms, you will be distracted by an array of inviting food in the delicatessen counter. You can sit in either of the two additional dining rooms and enjoy the hustle and bustle of happy eaters who greet each other like old friends.

Bonnie and Jay Silverman have owned Pumpernickles for three years. Their sons, Jake and Sam, are proudly part of the business's family image. Sam is away at college and helps out when he can. Jake, a friendly young man in his mid-teens, greets customers when they come in the door.

A PERSONAL NOTE:

Their secret of making the best matzo is to make sure it is moist before adding plenty of eggs. Yes, it can be done with just egg whites.

So where in St. Louis can you get matzo and eggs, called Matzo Byre? The dish is a favorite on the menu, and it is served with cinnamon sugar or syrup for $5.99. You may want to order a side of latkes — grilled potato pancakes. Mishagos, their famous corned beef hash, is served with two eggs and a bagel and is another big favorite.

Jay and Bonnie eagerly work the room greeting everyone and making sure they are taken care of. On one of the walls, you'll see framed photos of the families who frequent Pumpernickles. On another wall are photos of celebrities who have enjoyed the food. Preparing food for shivahs and catering bat and bar mitzvahs keeps the kitchen very busy, but they will deliver for all occasions.

When you have breakfast, you are sure to meet Frances Silverman, Jay's mother, and also Marilyn and Norman Shram, Bonnie's parents. This family wants to include you as well.

CONTACT INFO:
11036 Olive Street Rd.
St. Louis
314-567-4496
pumpernickles.com

Breakfast served all day!

SAUSAGE IS KING

The **Lewis Café** opened near the Frisco railroad tracks in St. Clair in 1936. Virgil Lewis took over the confectionary and started serving good homemade cooking in the downtown restaurant on the old Route 66.

The original charm and character has remained through the years. Seven oak booths and counter seating were all refurbished in 2004. It now is twice the size, thanks to current owner Chris Short, Virgil's great-nephew. Chris just so happens to raise his own Angus beef and hogs, guaranteeing fresh products for his café.

A PERSONAL NOTE:
The Lewis Café does not make their sausage from butchered scraps. They use the whole hog to make the very best quality.

Breakfast is big, and half of the breakfast business is biscuits and gravy. Whole-hog sausage is produced by slaughtering two hogs weekly to keep up with the restaurant's demand, as well as the take-home orders for sausage. The Ultimate Breakfast Sandwich, which includes a half-pound sausage patty, two eggs, hash browns, grilled onions, and cheese, is a popular item. Thick ham steaks are also a favorite. Sausage is evident in most menu items, but the café is also known for its amazing pies and Virgil's very own poppy seed celery dressing that he claims he got from a 1940s newspaper.

In the mornings, you'll find thirty women enjoying coffee in the main dining room. When it's time for them to leave, they pick up their husbands, who are having coffee in the counter room. The place then starts to fill with the lunch crowd. Six hundred cups of coffee are served each week.

Good sausage makes for good food and good company at this café.

"COFFEE SHOULD BE BLACK AS HELL, STRONG AS DEATH, AND SWEET AS LOVE."

— Turkish Proverb

Guest Check

CONTACT INFO:

145 S. Main St.

St. Clair

636-629-9975

Breakfast served all day!

CHECK NUMBER

№ 3605140

A CREATIVE BREAKFAST ESCAPE

The **Crooked Tree Coffee House** is named after a crooked tree growing on the grounds of nearby Lindenwood University. Located in the heart of St. Charles, this eclectic coffee house not only has a creative atmosphere, but a creative menu as well.

The morning clientele range from nearby university students to locals who want to enjoy a delicious breakfast. Coffee in many brewed flavors is offered as you wait at the counter to place your order. Healthy choices are plentiful on the menu, like the Spin Veggie Sandwich, which contains spinach, eggs, mushrooms, and feta and provolone cheese on a warm croissant. This comes with yogurt or fruit. The Breakfast Quesadilla, a big favorite, is made with sausage, sweet onions, tomatoes, and scallions and is served on a grilled flour tortilla. It has a zippier punch with the salsa and sour cream.

A PERSONAL NOTE:

Stein shares that there is a very small window of time to fix breakfast for customers. He creates an outline of every menu item and then the staff can put their own creative touches on them before serving. Employees personally present each order to the customers, hoping for a pleasing reaction and personal satisfaction.

Everything here is made from scratch, and the owner, Stein Hunter, is always trying new things on his loyal customers. His next experiment is a Chocolate Hazelnut Crème Blintz, made with nutella, cream cheese, and mixed berries. His ownership of eight years, and the coffee house's reputation of over thirty-five years, has the influence of making The Crooked Tree a fun place to work. "Laughing every day is a requirement to working here," Stein says. "If you care, it all comes!"

Comfy chairs, reading material, and the friendly atmosphere will encourage you to stay and have that second cup of coffee.

CONTACT INFO:

559 First Capitol Dr.

St. Charles

636-669-5282

crookedtreecoffee.com

Breakfast served all day!

A HAPPY FAMILY PLACE

What is red, yellow, and cute all over? It's the **Main Street Diner** in St. Peters. When John Grillo decided to open a diner, he put his sister in charge of decorating. She chose a coordinated vintage red-and-yellow theme for the décor, and it shows in the smallest of detail.

All of John's seven brothers and sisters became involved in some way. One brother did all the carpentry as well as some of the cooking. John's son cooks as well, and there are two nephews on staff.

The diner's location is a very busy corner on Main Street, near Interstate 70. The early morning breakfast crew blends in with the incoming lunch crowd.

The menu is very extensive, but John's own favorite is one of the scrambler selections. They are the Route 66, Aunt Katie's, and his favorite, Uncle John's. It combines three scrambled eggs with sausage, mushrooms, green peppers, onions, cheese, and fried potatoes. All the scrambler choices are $6.99. Many of the menu items are named after family, like Cousin Jeff's, which is two eggs over a medium biscuit on top of corned beef hash with gravy.

A PERSONAL NOTE:
The cook uses a Cajun seasoning on most breakfast dishes to give them a kick.

St. Peters has many surrounding farms that John likes to do business with. Fresh produce is key in planning his menu. If you are dining alone, you'll enjoy sitting at the counter, which has historic newspaper items glazed in for fun reading.

Sunday is reserved for breakfast eaters only — no lunch served. Everything here is happy: food, service, and atmosphere.

"WE MUST EAT TO LIVE AND LIVE TO EAT."

— Henry Fielding

Guest Check

CONTACT INFO:
315 Main St.
St. Peters
636-397-6260
mymainstreetdiner.com

CHECK NUMBER
No. 3605140

Breakfast served all day!

ALL IS NOT STONE

It has been just over a year since **Stone Soup Cottage** opened in Cottleville, but they have quickly established themselves not only for a fine dining experience, but for a fantastic brunch as well.

Carl and Nancy McConnell used their tourism background to open this small, charming restaurant that only accommodates twenty-four guests. Nancy and Carl grew up reading the children's tale *Stone Soup*, by Maria Brown. They thought the theme and name would be perfect for their European-style eatery, which is off the beaten path in St. Charles County.

The Chef's Tasting Brunch menu consists of five courses that are pre-planned for you. They are all served with precision, as well as a complimentary glass of champagne or a mimosa. The first course is fruit and yogurt sorbet, followed by your choice of eggs benedict or a petit omelet. The third course offers custard cinnamon French toast or a buttermilk crêpe. The fourth course changes the palette completely with beef tenderloin medallions with Burgundy wine and chanterelle mushrooms. Your other choice for that course is the fresh seafood of the day. The fifth course is the finishing-touch dessert of crème brûlée and berries.

Carl purchases sixty-eight different varieties of produce that are available from their next-door neighbor and farmer, Norman Wiese.

The brunch experience is enhanced by the personal service. Carl and Nancy visit with each and every patron, and they acknowledge all their repeat customers by name. As you can imagine, reservations are required long in advance.

Guest Check

CONTACT INFO:

SERVER   TABLE   GUESTS   CHECK NUMBER

№ 3605140

5525 Oak St.

Cottleville

636-244-2233

stonesoupcottage.com

BRUNCH ON SUNDAY

BREAKFAST FOR ALL!

Having breakfast at **Lady Di's Diner** is a social experience for all. Just ask the "Sex and the City Girls" who have breakfast there every Saturday morning at 8:30. This group of former nurses, who are loyal customers, were given this nickname by the employees of the diner. These ladies know how to have fun and take frequent trips in one of the girls' red convertible.

The girls will be happy to share their favorites on the menu — though they order the same thing each week, even though there are thirty-eight menu items to choose from. Diane Sago, who opened the diner in 1996, has gotten to know the girls well and has their orders ready to go.

A PERSONAL NOTE:

Diane advises flipping the eggs, and she likes to use a flat grill to make her omelets. She loves to tell the story of making hamburgers for all of President Obama's staff when they visited St. Charles.

A nice seasonal plus to this small diner is the covered patio with seating for sixty. Diane is energetic and works the room inside and out, greeting everyone by name. Smokers and large groups of regulars, like the local firemen, pull up in their trucks and find their seats on the picnic benches.

Omelets are huge here — in size and in popularity. They can be made with any number of eggs that you choose. The size of the biggest one is made of thirteen eggs, and no doubt it is shared by more than one eater. The Half Lady Di's Omelet on the menu is long, high, and overwhelming to consume. It's made of ham, green peppers, onions, and eggs on top of a big serving of hash browns. It's then smothered with chili and topped with cheese. More than two can certainly share, and the price can't be beat at $8.50.

The Pancake Sandwich is something to note. The pancakes hold two eggs and two strips of bacon, so you get the whole breakfast effect in one bite.

Lady Di's Diner is everything a good diner should be, and more.

CONTACT INFO:
620 N. Kingshighway St.
St. Charles
636-916-4442
ladydisdiner.com

Breakfast served all day!

A ST. LOUIS TRADITION

You can't talk about breakfast in the St. Louis region without mentioning **Uncle Bill's Pancake House**.

In 1961, Bill Ernst ended his career as a used-car salesman and converted the former Medart's Restaurant into St. Louis's first pancake house. It wasn't long before he purchased the lot next door, just to handle all the parking for his successful new business.

Betty Kraus, the current manager, started working as a waitress in 1964, and she can tell you about every breakfast item and how timing is so important in serving all their customers over the years. Waitresses are trained to carry as many as eight plates on their left arms: flat foods on bottom and fluffier dishes on top.

Breakfast is 70 percent of the day's sales.

A PERSONAL NOTE:

One of their best-kept secrets is their special cut of Oscar Mayer bacon. It is cut extra thick, and they go through twenty to twenty-five cases a week. People remember quality products like this.

There are fourteen kinds of pancakes to choose from, or you can request your own combination. Betty said people sometimes request many unusual condiments and syrups. One lady requested mustard, and another asked to sample every pancake the restaurant offers. We must not overlook the waffles. There are five great choices, but the talk of the town is the Alaska, topped with ice cream and pure fudge sauce. It's a sight to behold.

The regular customers with unusual requests are noted on the ticket when they order. The cook knows who it is for and how to prepare it.

Many self-seaters, as they are called, go directly to their seats instead of waiting for the hostess. Locals love to introduce their friends and family to this St. Louis tradition, just as they do with Ted Drewes frozen custard.

There are two locations of this St. Louis original to please twice as many folks.

CONTACT INFO:
3427 S. Kingshighway Blvd.
St. Louis
314-832-1973

14196 Manchester Rd.
Manchester
314-394-1416

Breakfast served all day!

NO. 3605140

A BREAKFAST CORNER

For more than sixty years, **Spencer's Grill** has provided a healthy breakfast for its neighbors, local officials, and regional celebrities like Cardinals baseball players. The location is a busy corner in the charming community of Kirkwood, and it has become a local landmark.

Chris Powers, owner of seven years, keeps traffic moving in this small forty-one-seat diner. Family members also put in hours behind the grill and counter.

Spencer's is one of few local diners that serve Scrapple. This dish originated in Pennsylvania. It is traditionally made of a mush of pork and trimmings combined with cornmeal, flour, and spices. Square in shape, it is usually covered with gravy, or syrup if you prefer. A slightly healthier choice is their blueberry pancakes. The very fresh berries explode in your mouth, which makes them the most frequently ordered item on the menu.

A PERSONAL NOTE:

The diner loves to brag about their delicious coffee. Coffee is brewed fresh in a timely manner for their customers.

They were also voted best biscuits and gravy in St. Louis by *St. Louis Diner Review* in 2007.

The diner's reputation started as one of the frequent stops on Route 66. It has been featured in two movies, *Chatelaine*, where a vampire ate breakfast, and *How I Got Lost*.

If you have to wait for a seat, which would not be unusual, the friendly staff will offer you coffee and make your wait worthwhile.

CONTACT INFO:

SERVER   TABLE   GUESTS

223 S. Kirkwood Rd.   CHECK NUMBER

NO. 3605140

Kirkwood

314-821-2601

Breakfast served all day!

HAVE A BIKE AND A BITE

The Frenchtown Historic District in St. Charles is the perfect location for the **2nd Street Bike Stop Café**. Just one block west is the Katy Trail and one block south is the Blanchette boat dock. Where else are you going to get your bicycle gear while you grab a wonderful breakfast to start your day?

Jodi Devonshire and Tony Caruso paired up to do what they each do best. The combination of biking and food make it a perfect tourist destination.

Jodi brags about their all-natural menu that uses local farm produce, as well as her own homegrown garden food and Companion bread, which is baked just miles away. The menu choices are cleverly named after bike themes — like the Triathlon Wrap, which is three cheeses melted over eggs, tomatoes, mushrooms, drizzled with ranch dressing, then grilled to a golden brown. The Breakaway is a surprisingly large bowl of homemade oatmeal topped with fresh blueberries and strawberries.

A PERSONAL NOTE:

The owners want you to know the value of composting. They practice it for their garden, and it reduces their waste by 95 percent.

Gooey Butter Cake, for which the St. Louis region is famous, can also be found here as a great dessert or a great afternoon pit stop. The espresso menu has it all, from iced delights to steamy hot choices.

The colorful ceramic designs in their wrought-iron table and chairs add a feminine touch to soften the other side of the café, which reminds you that is it also a bike shop. So roll in for a bike tune-up and enjoy a mocha latte.

CONTACT INFO:
1325 N. 2nd St.
St. Charles
636-724-9900
2ndstreetbikestopcafe.webs.com

Breakfast served all day!

A TASTE OF IRELAND

Erin's Coffee Shoppe is certain to take you back to Ireland for your breakfast experience. Maggi and Sid Ritchie immigrated to Canada from Ireland sixteen years ago. When they retired, they landed in Winfield and decided to open a restaurant with Irish influences. Maggi and Sid named the restaurant after their granddaughter Erin who lives in London, Ontario.

The dining room, café, and parlor are known as the Home of the Ulster Fry—a signature dish on their extensive menu. For only $6.95, the full plate consists of two farm-fresh eggs, cooked medium soft, three softly fried Irish breads, potato farl, soda farl, two links of sausage, two slices of bacon, fried tomatoes, mushrooms, and one pancake. They soon hope to have a video of how to make this on their website. Farl is from the Gaelic word *fardel* and is a quarter section of a round that has been cooked for about three minutes on each side.

A PERSONAL NOTE:
A secret ingredient to Maggi's delicious Irish cooking is a finely ground white pepper that is a special blend they import from Ireland.

Maggi said all the recipes used for their all-day menu are from their grandmothers and mothers. They are proud to support local farmers like Winfield's and Brown Smoke House for all their meats.

Enticing coffee selections are also available, so I say, "Top of the morning to ya, from Erin's."

"I JUDGE A RESTAURANT
BY THE BREAD AND BY THE
COFFEE."

—Burt Lancaster

Guest Check

CONTACT INFO:

SERVER	TABLE	GUESTS	CHECK NUMBER

201 Main St.   № 3605140
Winfield
636-566-8316
erinscoffee.com

Breakfast served all day!

AN OMELET RECORD

For less than ten dollars, you will be sure to enjoy a good breakfast at **Tony's West Restaurant**, conveniently located in a strip mall in the southwestern part of St. Charles. Tony's has been owned for the last four years by Dan and Debbie Strantz.

Breakfast is the busiest time for this neighborhood eatery that caters to the many residents of its nearby subdivisions. The smoking side of the place is where you will see the grill with very busy cooks behind the counter. Hungry customers sitting at the counter watch the activity as they converse with familiar faces. The second room has tables filled with families enjoying their breakfasts.

The menu is full of varied breakfast choices. The big brag is that they claim to have the record for making the largest omelet in the state of Missouri. That would be an omelet made with twenty-five eggs, and which is so big it has to be served on a pizza pan. Debbie's father conceived the idea when he first owned the restaurant in St. Louis County.

A PERSONAL NOTE:

Dan brags about how much people love his hash browns. He melts real butter on the grill before he adds potatoes to create really crispy hash browns.

On the reverse side of things, you may want to try Guy's Low Carb Breakfast, made with a beef patty, topped with two pieces of bacon, mushrooms, and cheese on a bed of lettuce.

Offering later hours, this is a great place to have that late-night breakfast that you crave after a long day or evening. You may not be up to the twenty-five-egg omelet, but there are other favorites you will love at Tony's.

"WE SELDOM REPORT OF HAVING EATEN TOO LITTLE."
— Thomas Jefferson

CONTACT INFO:
1009 Wolfrum Rd.
St. Charles
636-329-8985

CHECK NUMBER
N⁰ 3605140

Breakfast served all day!

THE NAME SAYS IT ALL

The **Ham N' Egg Family Restaurant** is a busy, home-style eatery with a golden décor, reminding you that you are there to enjoy eggs. The coordinated bright-striped tablecloths create a happy atmosphere. It is somewhat hidden in the city of O'Fallon. It is in the Crossing Plaza behind the Walgreen's at the intersection of the busy roads K and N.

Chad and Chris Ozdinc are the rookie owners of this place. Chris is the cook. Chad's wife, Valerie, is one of the many cheerful employees who greet you when you arrive.

The appetizing menu's best-selling item is the Double Up Breakfast. It consists of two eggs, four strips of bacon or sausage links, two slices of French toast, and their famous home fries. These fries

A PERSONAL NOTE:

What makes their home fries so good is that they cut them fresh from potatoes like you do at home and make them in a skillet instead of a grill.

come with most entrées, and the waitresses always stress their popularity when customers are ordering. The buttermilk pancakes are made from their own secret recipe. They are light and fluffy for sure. For an interesting twist, order the Pigs in a Blanket, which is three sausage links wrapped in those fluffy pancakes. Six hot skillet choices are available with all your breakfast favorites. Six delightful omelets are offered on the menu, accompanied by home fries, toast, and jelly.

There are a couple of outdoor picnic tables on the sidewalk if you have to wait for a seat inside. In nice weather, you can also be served outdoors.

"LIFE WITHIN DOORS HAS FEW PLEASANTER PROSPECTS THAN A NEATLY ARRANGED AND WELL-PROVISIONED BREAKFAST TABLE."
— Nathaniel Hawthorne

Guest Check

CHECK NUMBER
№ 3605140

CONTACT INFO:
2924 Hwy. K
O'Fallon
636-272-3898
hamneggrestaurant.com

Breakfast served all day!

SUNRISE ON THE HILL

If you want breakfast early or late in the day on the Hill, you will soon discover **Chris' Pancake and Dining**.

Owner Chris Saracino comes from a family engrained in the restaurant business.

In 1987, his father owned Bartolino's, a well-known Italian Restaurant, and now his other two sons operate Bartolino's South and Bartolino's Osteria. Chris's leadership and restaurant legacy earned him the presidency of the Hill Business Association. They also sponsor the Camp Wyman Charity Golf Tournament.

The most popular item at Chris' is the King of the Hill, which is two eggs over a hamburger topped with hash browns, cheddar cheese, and onions, served with pancakes or toast. The health-conscious customer can enjoy the wheat and honey waffles or buckwheat pancakes with sugar-free syrup.

A PERSONAL NOTE:

Their business card says, "Cook good food & give plenty." Chris knows how important this is and feels they live up to their mission.

Local customers make up 60 percent of the clientele that keep Chris busy greeting tables around the four nicely designed dining rooms. This personal touch is one of the reasons Chris has been so successful. Saracino family members have also served throughout the years with other longtime employees.

This traditional family is important to this Italian historic area and to St. Louis folks who continue to bring their friends and family to enjoy a great breakfast.

"BREAKFAST IS A FORECAST OF THE WHOLE DAY: SPOIL THAT AND ALL IS SPOILED."

— Leigh Hunt

CONTACT INFO:

5980 Southwest Ave.

St. Louis

314-645-2088

bartolinosrestaurants.com

Breakfast served all day!

CHECK NUMBER

NO. 3605140

A LITTLE DOUGH AND A LOT OF PASSION

Brother and sister Josh and Jodi Allen started **Companion** in 1993. It now has two locations and a bakery outlet, not to mention the many restaurants and stores that serve Companion bread. Where else would you consider ordering toast for your main breakfast item?

Breakfast at Companion Café is not only about the variety of breads, pretzels, and pastries, it's also about their Baked Eggs. The two-inch-high delight melts in your mouth. They come in three different choices of ingredients. Their famous toast comes with baked eggs, or you can have a dish of fruit instead. Café Oatmeal lovers enjoy the oatmeal made from scratch that comes with many delicious toppings like chopped apricots. Other healthy choices include the Granola and Yogurt Parfait and the Smoked Salmon on a Bagel. Companion is pleased to purchase many products from local farmers like Patchwork Farms.

The outdoor seating is very popular at the Clayton location. The busy streetscape is entertaining in itself. In

A PERSONAL NOTE:

They are more than happy to share their Baked Egg recipe on their website, as well as a helpful video that shows you how to make your very own.

South St. Louis, Companion opens their factory/bakery for the public on Friday, Saturday, and Sunday. The Early Bird Outlet on Gustine Avenue has been a bonus to the many outlet vendors that sell the famous bread.

There's nothing like lovin' from the oven at Companion Bread!

Guest Check

SERVER	TABLE	GUESTS	CHECK NUMBER

CONTACT INFO: N⁰ 3605140

8143 Maryland Ave.
Clayton
314-352-4770
companionstl.com

A MEDITERRANEAN FLAIR

When you visit the **Boardwalk Café** in Webster Groves, be prepared for a wonderful breakfast with a Mediterranean twist. This influence comes from owner of four years, Ismail Ilhan. He migrated from Turkey in 1990 and found his place in the kitchen, doing what he loves best.

The charming community is pleased to have this award-winning café listed as one of the best by the *Riverfront Times* in St. Louis. In 2009, they were rated fourth as the overall best breakfast, and they came in second for having the best omelets and second in pancakes.

Ismail named one of his omelet choices the Webster Omelet. It has three eggs, chicken gyro meat, onions, tomatoes, jalapeños, spinach, mushrooms, and feta cheese. It is served with their home fries and toast. The Mediterranean Omelet is similar, only with beef and minus the spinach and jalapeños. Ten other omelet choices are available if these are not to your liking. Nine different skillet breakfasts are very popular, and customers can create their own combinations as well.

You will feel the small-town atmosphere when you visit. The seniors from the nearby condo development provide more than 60 percent of the Boardwalk's clientele.

A PERSONAL NOTE:

Three things to note here: Omelets should be flipped within ten to fifteen seconds; no can openers used here, as all items are fresh; and they only hire the best servers to help you.

Whether you are there to eat breakfast or lunch, the Mediterranean flare will make the Boardwalk Café stand out.

CONTACT INFO:

CHECK NUMBER

N°. 2605140

600 E. Lockwood Ave.

Webster Groves

314-963-0013

boardwalkcafestl.com

Breakfast served all day!

A CIVIL WAR STOP

Every three years, the residents of Arcadia Valley remember the Battle of Pilot Knob at Fort Davidson. It is a large tourist attraction that draws visitors from all over the country, especially Civil War historians. Directly across the street from this historic site is the **Fort Davidson Restaurant**. Phyllis Kennedy Sharp purchased the restaurant in 1991 after working for the previous owner.

The three large rooms with a country décor can seat two hundred people, allowing for small parties. Murals, painted by Jo Buffalo, depict the different themes of the battle. Tourists can mingle with the locals who occupy the tables on a daily basis.

A PERSONAL NOTE:

Phyllis feels their success comes from being consistent with their cooking procedures. When the cooks change, which can be frequent in this business, Phyllis makes sure the preparations do not, so customers are not disappointed.

Breakfast is kept simple, but Phyllis said her mixture for French toast is one of the most popular dishes. It's referred to as Golden French Toast on the menu under the Sweet Tooth section and is just $3.29. Phyllis is also proud of the white gravy, which has a unique texture perfect for many menu choices. She uses fresh produce when available, and she always makes sure fresh fruit of some kind is on hand. Many specials are served daily. For just $4.29, you can enjoy two eggs your way, bacon, hash browns, and biscuits—which is a bargain to be sure.

There are many things from history, nature, and art to enjoy at this café in the heart of Missouri.

"TO EAT IS HUMAN, TO DIGEST DIVINE."
—Charles T. Copeland

CONTACT INFO:
210 S. McCune St.
Pilot Knob
573-546-2719

CHECK NUMBER
N9 3605140

LIMITED BREAKFAST HOURS

SISTERS IN KIND

When Diana Abernathy talked her sister Darla Macke into managing her diner, **The Pie Bird Café**, she wasn't sure about bringing in family. Now there are at least six family members doing different jobs for her in this busy small-town diner in Fruitland.

Diane received a pie bird as a gift, which gave her the idea for the name. A ceramic pie bird was traditionally placed in the center of a pie to release the steam when baking. The theme took off and now you will see a collection of pie birds on shelves inside the diner. Pie is indeed on many people's minds when they visit, and there are many options.

Folks from the surrounding community enjoy breakfast here every day. The Hash Brown Casserole is a side dish choice with many breakfast items, but folks love to order it as a main course, as they also often do with the macaroni and cheese. The hash browns' very cheesy taste consists of cream of chicken soup, sour cream, onions, a combination of seasonings, and lots of hash browns.

Their homemade pecan or walnut waffles also get high marks along with the daily special of two eggs, meat choice, fried potatoes, hash brown casserole or grits, half-order of biscuits and gravy, and toast for just $6.59.

This mini diner was once a gas station. The counter in front of the cooking area has only four stools. Tables throughout the place have had legs confiscated from old sewing machines. The food, charm, and friendly atmosphere say a lot for this sisterhood diner.

CONTACT INFO:

5512 U.S. Hwy. 61

Jackson

573-243-4788

Breakfast served all day!

BREAKFAST BY WILLOW POND

Perryville, Missouri, is fortunate to have the **Willow House Bed and Breakfast** alongside a lovely pond that you can see right outside the window.

It is Perryville's first bed-and-breakfast, owned and operated by David and Karen Pierce. David is a PGA golfer employed at the Perryville Country Club, and Karen excels in music and sings in the choir at the Cathedral Basilica in St. Louis. Karen also excels in the kitchen with her large collection of recipes. She loves choosing David's favorites and experimenting with new ideas.

A PERSONAL NOTE:

Karen serves her own rosemary-infused syrup at all meals. The clear combination of honey, rosemary, water, and sugar complement fruit or dessert. Her discovery has been a big hit with guests.

Most guests enjoy baked egg dishes in puff pastry that come with a generous tray of melons and other fruits. Her blueberry muffins with a sugar glaze are the perfect complement to most of the dishes she serves. The Pierces love hosting private parties where they can create an array of hors d'oeuvres.

Sit-down dinners are perfect for this environment, and both David and Karen love to host them. Girls' craft weekends are also getting a lot of attention. Besides the great accommodations, an excellent dinner and breakfast, a free shuttle service is extended to local wineries, and a picnic basket can be arranged. This is all-inclusive for just fifty-four dollars per person.

Lovely understated bedrooms, comfortable sitting rooms, and the delicious breakfast make for a great visit. Oh, did I mention a complimentary bag of bread crumbs is available for when you go feed the ducks on the lake?

CONTACT INFO:

220 E. North St.

Perryville

573-547-9900

willowhousebandb.com

LIMITED BREAKFAST HOURS

A GERMAN DELIGHT

Farmington, Missouri, is a delightful community and the home of the Francis County seat. Across from the courthouse is **Bauhaus Kaffee**. This roomy, restored restaurant is a delightful place to have breakfast as you look out the large front windows. Beautiful hardwood floors display clusters of comfortable tables, chairs, and couches.

The walls are graced with tasteful posters done by Unique Ink. They artistically portray all the musical events that take place at the café.

Pat Antonowitsch Bennett, the owner, is of German descent and brings the taste of Germany to her menu choices—especially the baked goods. Her husband, Jon, is also involved in this two-year-old venture.

A PERSONAL NOTE:

When you are making exceptional scones, remember not to overwork the dough. Use frozen shredded butter, leaving chunks of butter visible before baking.

The hand-baked scones are a signature delight to be ordered with most of the coffee choices shown on the order board above the counter. Four different flavors of scones are offered, but the raspberry white chocolate scones sell the best. Other popular breakfast choices are their quiches. The combinations vary each day, except the Quiche Lorraine. The richest and most unusual quiche by far is the Feta Leek. The leeks are sautéed before they are combined with the quiche custard, and then yummy feta cheese is added. The light crust makes it an amazing combination for your taste buds.

It's a destination restaurant that has earned its advertising slogan as "Southeast Missouri's finest Coffee House and Restaurant."

CONTACT INFO:
9 N. Jefferson St.
Farmington
573-756-4555
bauhauskaffee.com

Breakfast served all day!

BREAKFAST WITH ROSES

The **Rose Bed Inn** is very versatile in its offerings and eclectic in its appearance. Eldon Nattier and James Coley, the proprietors, own one block of six buildings for their hospitality business. The oldest is a 1908 brick home, once owned by William Schrader, a prominent brick contractor. The location rests along the Mississippi River in the historic town of Cape Girardeau. The widow's walk on the roof offers a splendid view of the river and the town.

This bed-and-breakfast is known throughout the state for having superb food, especially for breakfast. The presentation is creative and delicious, just like the other dining experiences they offer. Breakfast usually starts with yogurt topped with their recipe of granola mix. Compotes of fresh fruit are then presented before the main course. Most folks prefer the generous light omelets that Chef James carefully prepares with herbs from their outdoor gardens. Potatoes, sausage, and toast are great complements to this wholesome meal.

> A PERSONAL NOTE:
>
> Chef James's hint for making lighter and fluffier omelets is to use heavy whipping cream and whip with an immersion blender.

Chef James's reputation has been acknowledged and his talents awarded. He loves teaching his cooking classes in the formal dining room. He tells his students "not to listen to their mama, and play with their food." His culinary creativity has inspired many.

Eldon's role is to manage the properties and all the events for the Rose Bed Inn.

CONTACT INFO:

611 S. Sprigg St.

Cape Girardeau

573-332-7673

rosebedinn.com

LIMITED BREAKFAST HOURS

BREAKFAST ON THE BLUFFS

Brian Helms, owner of the **White Cliff Manor Bed and Breakfast** in St. Mary's, claims he just serves a good ol' American breakfast each morning. I say it's far above average because so much thought and preparation go into each and every dish. The dish presentation in the formal dining room of this magnificent home is impressive.

Preparing what's in season is important, so the first taste is usually fresh berries from local farmers, followed by local sausage and a rich omelet. Fresh homemade biscuits are made each morning and served with special English preserves that Brian imports, and which you can buy along with many other items in the gift shop. Yes, there's English tea. So, there goes the all-American breakfast.

A PERSONAL NOTE:

Brian purchases local free-range chicken eggs because the yolks are high, orange, and perform the best. When he purchases fresh local sausage, he also adds his own sage and spices to make it to his own style and taste.

Brian takes breakfast to another level with the Deluxe Champagne Breakfast. He's happy to serve the lavish array of courses to you right in your room or on the large porch that overlooks the bluffs. The offerings include a filet mignon with any style of eggs, O'Brien potatoes, fresh fruit compote, and assorted Danishes.

The 1879 registered historic home was once owned by

a prosperous miller. The rooms are furnished with comfortable and tasteful antiques. The large front and back porches are most inviting as you view the gardens and hillsides that overlook 15,000 acres of Kaskaskia Island Bottoms.

In the backyard, you'll want to visit the Tea Gift Box, which was once a smokehouse. Inside, you will see English china sets, teapots, vases, and platters displayed with English lemon curd, teas, and preserves, ready to purchase for your trip home. Friendly outdoor cats, dogs, and a mellow horse peering over the fence will greet you when you drive up to this ten-acre estate.

Dinners and special-occasion events can also be arranged at this elegant home away from home.

Guest Check

CONTACT INFO:

SERVER   TABLE   GUEST   CHECK NUMBER

200 Second St.   N⁰ 3605140

St. Mary's

573-543-5445

whitecliffmanorbnb.com

LIMITED BREAKFAST HOURS

IN THE KITCHEN WITH DIANA

Carl and Diana Fuhring opened **Diana's Diner** in downtown St. James five years ago, and it continues to be a favorite stop—especially for breakfast. Diana loves to cook and is in charge of the kitchen, and Carl takes care of the restaurant's car theme. Carl has always loved cars, so he organizes an annual October car show called Diana's Old Car Show. It's great for the diner's business and great fun for car enthusiasts.

Diana is proud of her own breakfast creation, Diana's Special. On the grill she mixes together hash browns, onions, eggs, and diced country ham, topped with cheese and served with toast or biscuits. It's a big favorite for only $5.25 and guaranteed to fill you up. For your sweet tooth, Diana's plate-sized cinnamon rolls are the talk of the town, along with her delicious homemade pies. You can enjoy unlimited coffee with both.

A PERSONAL NOTE:

When making home-made biscuits, sprinkle in raisins or nuts in the dough. Add a touch of almond extract to make a tastier icing on the top.

The diner is conscious of using fresh produce when available, which shows in their fresh-quality food. Two counters and seats for a hundred await your visit. Whether it is breakfast or cars you're interested in, drive up and check it out.

"THE MORNING CUP OF COFFEE HAS AN EXHILARATION ABOUT IT WHICH THE CHEERING INFLUENCE OF THE AFTERNOON OR EVENING CUP OF TEA CANNOT BE EXPECTED TO REPRODUCE."

—Oliver Wendall Holmes, 1888

Guest Check

CONTACT INFO:

103 N. Jefferson St.

St. James

866-488-9078

dianasdiner.com

CHECK NUMBER

NO. 3605140

LIMITED BREAKFAST HOURS

A STE. GENEVIEVE LANDMARK

The **Southern Hotel Bed and Breakfast**, which was established around 1875 in Ste. Genevieve, is the longest-operating lodging establishment west of the Mississippi River. The Federal-style building was built in the 1790s.

Mike and Cathy Hankins have owned this bed-and-breakfast for more than twenty-five years. They have claimed numerous awards that place them in the top three B&Bs in Missouri, and they have been listed as one of the most romantic B&Bs in the state.

Each room is embellished in Victorian style and collections of items, like fans and spoons, are displayed in almost every room. It also has a game room that has a functional 1875 pool table. There is no chance of being bored in the Southern Hotel.

The eleven guest rooms can handle twenty-two people and includes a "quilt room" where seventeen quilts are loaded with signatures, starting with the very first guests. The backyard gardens are lush with flowers and lawn ornaments to entertain strollers along a winding path.

The food preparation is a high priority. They carry a full restaurant license and have a professional kitchen

> **A PERSONAL NOTE:**
> Attached to the hotel is an additional surprise. Mike has created an art gallery where he sells the work of the "Best of Missouri Hands." There are thirty-nine artists whose media represent everything from art glass to garments.

with the latest equipment. Their signature dish is Amish Friendship Bread with a touch of butterscotch. A Crustless Spinach Quiche, Blueberry French Toast, and the Overnight O'Brian are the guests' favorites. All come with apple wedges or orange slices with caramel sauce.

They are well prepared for folks who need to have gluten-free breads, cereals, and main dishes. Organic foods are purchased in the summer from the farmers' market just down the street.

The Southern Hotel is not only a feast for your eyes but for your morning appetite as well.

CONTACT INFO:
146 S. 3rd St.
Ste. Genevieve
800-275-1412
southernhotelbb.com

CHECK NUMBER
No 3605140

LIMITED BREAKFAST HOURS

PARK AND EAT

Longtime residents in Perryville may remember when the **Park-et Fine Foods** location was a tractor dealership.

On heavily traveled Highway 61 (also known as Kingshighway), Herb Lukafur had a vision of opening a restaurant with a motel next door, so he named it in reference to parking your car and eating. The modern, flat-roof, vintage building is lined with large windows on three sides, so you can view all the activity of folks coming and going.

In 1991, Kevin and Brenda Esselman purchased the restaurant and have not looked back. They know the good homestyle food needs to be consistent to please their following through past generations.

A PERSONAL NOTE:

The Esselmans try to find out what the locals like best and keep the menu consistent with the best quality, so no matter when they visit, they know what to expect.

Homemade pies have always been their signature attraction. Margie Hudson, Brenda's mother, helps bake the pies and eats many of her meals at the counter along with other regular customers. Breakfast is a big deal with Perryville's early risers. Brenda brags about making homemade fresh biscuits and gravy each day, which has earned them the Best in Perry County Award for their special gravy.

All prices are reasonable, like the Large Breakfast

Special. Two eggs, hash browns, a meat choice, and toast cannot be beat for just $4.99. The country ham, chosen most often, is purchased locally from Stonie's Sausage and Meats.

The town of 6,000 folks will encourage you to come "park it" and meet with all the locals for breakfast.

"EAT NOT TO DULLNESS. DRINK NOT TO ELEVATION."

— Benjamin Franklin

Guest Check

CONTACT INFO:
211 S. Kingshighway
Perryville
573-547-4147

Breakfast served all day!

CHECK NUMBER

N⁰ 3605140

PANCAKES, STEAK, OR BOTH

Rolla, located in central Missouri, is known throughout the state for the Missouri University of Science and Technology (previously known as University of Missouri at Rolla) that originated in 1870. If you ask the locals where you can get a good breakfast, they will tell you that **Zeno's Motel and Steakhouse** is the place to check out. In 1957, Zeno Scheffer opened this popular eatery, now run by third-generation owners Mike and Tracy Scheffer. Other family members also work at this sizable restaurant that serves more than three hundred people daily.

Even though its "steak house" reputation is huge, along with its motel/inn, you will want to start your day at this Route 66 breakfast stop. What do patrons love at Zeno's? No question: the dinner-plate-sized pancakes have everyone talking. Tracy's Favorite is the blueberry pancakes, which are light and fluffy and made the old-fashioned way with lots of blueberries and real butter. A Breakfast Buffet can be set up for any group of twenty-five or more.

A PERSONAL NOTE:

The owners say, "Our personal service is important in all we do! This is what we are known for. Our customers expect it, and we want every visit to be as good as the last!"

Like so many good eateries, getting fresh produce is essential to their entire menu. For breakfast, lunch, or dinner, and even their overnight services, Zeno's will take care of you.

"ONLY DULL PEOPLE ARE BRILLIANT AT BREAKFAST."

— Oscar Wilde

CONTACT INFO:

CHECK NUMBER

N9 0605140

1621 Martin Springs Dr.

Rolla

573-364-1301

zenos.biz

LIMITED BREAKFAST HOURS

BRING YOUR APPETITE

In 2004, Elaine Rundell took her many years of restaurant experience and teamed up with her daughter Lisa Shockley in a business venture. Lisa had an accounting background along with "people personality" to make them the perfect duo. The **Country Café** in Festus is the place to go for a good country breakfast. Plan on eating with the locals; they know no strangers. You will see them there early and late.

Generous servings show up on your plate, no matter what you order. The Big Kid's Breakfast is enough for any adult. Three slices of bacon or sausage, one egg, hash browns, and toast should be big enough for any kid. If you're really hungry, order the Big Boy, which includes

A PERSONAL NOTE:

Farm-fresh products from the nearby farmers are something they take pride in. Elaine's theory of not cutting any corners when it comes to cooking and good food are paying off.

an eight-ounce country-fried steak, sixteen-ounce country ham, or two pork chops, three eggs, home fries, and toast for $10.99. I hear the Breakfast Burrito with home fries is more than hot, because of the jalapeños. Six different kinds of omelets are available to choose from. Three eggs can be combined with any of your favorite foods. There actually is something healthy on the menu. The Light and Lean includes two eggs of your choice, a cup of fruit, and whole-wheat toast for just $3.99.

Oh, and pies. Did I mention the pies? Lisa is a baker of at least ten different kinds of pie, and some are nearly the mile high they claim they are. You will see them displayed by the front door; it's a tempting reminder that you can take one home.

The Country Café is an easy stop right off the main highway, located in a small strip mall, and well worth the visit.

Guest Check

CONTACT INFO:

CHECK NUMBER

N⁰ 3605140

2561 U.S. Hwy. 67

Festus

636-931-5805

Breakfast served all day!

ROCK 'N' ROLL BREAKFAST

You can step back in the 1950s or 1960s if you make a breakfast stop at the **Grillz Diner** in Sikeston. Owner Frank Faraci has a background in restaurants but decided on the "diner" concept in 2009. His experience and passion show in his menu. Some recipes he uses are from his early life in Connecticut.

The Cadillac is for the many hungry folks who look forward to three eggs, bacon, sausage, and hash browns, all served in a hot skillet with a side order of a pancake. If you have room for toast, it's there as well. Frank says his oatmeal is the best around. He makes it with milk instead of water, adds cinnamon, a little pumpkin spice, and covers it with maple syrup. If you love pancakes, you should consider the Banana Pancake. It will cover your entire plate and is light and tasty because he adds smashed bananas, pumpkin spice, cinnamon, and crushed walnuts.

A PERSONAL NOTE:

When making pancakes, make your skillet very, very hot and lightly spray with oil, not butter. Use half-and-half with scrambled eggs and cook them slowly in a skillet, not on a grill.

Wimberly Farms is across the street from the diner, and Frank is one of their best customers. He is the first to get fresh produce.

You can enjoy sitting and chatting at the diner counter, a cozy booth, or one of the tables—if you can find an empty one, that is. Whether you're there for a good breakfast, the 1950s music, or nostalgia, "Be there or be square."

CONTACT INFO:
2600 E. Malone Ave.
Sikeston
573-471-3211

Breakfast served all day!

INN GIVES BACK

There's more than meets the mouth at the **Du Kum Inn** in Sullivan, a town of 6,000 folks that straddles the border of Franklin and Crawford counties. Theresa Hulsey and her sister Mary Blankenship are just part of the eight family members who cook and serve at this restaurant that promises to continue for generations. The restaurant originated fifty years ago, but the inn has been at this location for seventeen years.

Breakfast gets a lot of attention at this popular stop because of its good homemade cooking. They feel they have bragging rights on their biscuits and gravy, which are made from scratch. Hash browns made from real potatoes are little things that matter with the folks who eat here day after day.

Omelets and more omelets are ordered every day — seven different kinds to be exact. You will most likely get to try their tasty hash browns, because they come with most breakfast entrées. You might also want to have pie for breakfast, because the pies are most delicious here. There is only one other choice that is more popular, and that's their bread pudding. Thick portions of bread are

> **A PERSONAL NOTE:**
>
> This family's history of giving back with their success started with their father, who always provided a free breakfast on game day for the high school football team. In time, the girls were also included during softball season, and they too receive a free breakfast on game day. This is a win-win for their customers and the town of Sullivan.

combined with cinnamon, eggs, and milk. That's all topped with their own vanilla sauce. It consists of rich cream, vanilla, sugar, and butter. So if you decide to start with one of these delightful sweets, instead of waiting for dessert, you have my permission.

The Du Kum Inn is a great place to bring your family for an affordable breakfast. Their slogan, "Come in as a stranger, and leave as friends," makes it worth checking out.

Guest Check

CHECK NUMBER

NO 3605140

CONTACT INFO:
101 Grande Center
Sullivan
573-468-6114

LIMITED BREAKFAST HOURS

GOOD SECRETS SHOULD BE KEPT

When you meet the owner of **Myrtle's Place** in Poplar Bluff, she will share her interesting history of the diner, but don't ask for any of the restaurant's tips or recipes. Debbie Sliger was a waitress at this diner for eleven years and learned the ropes. She knew when she walked into the place years ago that she would own it some day, and so it goes. As the owner for fourteen years, Debbie has made this a real family enterprise. Her mother, who is eighty-five, a sister, niece, daughter, and daughter-in-law all serve the diner in some way. Debbie says that everyone gets along, on most days, which is something to be proud of.

Debbie does 80 percent of the cooking. Most of the recipes are in her head. The Debbie Special is the most frequently ordered dish. It is a choice of meat, hash browns, and two biscuits and gravy. Speaking of

A PERSONAL NOTE:

Debbie thinks there should be a "secret" in every good thing a great cook makes. So don't ask the cook for her secrets.

hash browns, her Hash Brown Delight is a unique side dish, but also a filling and delicious entrée. The potatoes are mixed with onions, tomatoes, peppers, and cheese. Egg Scramblers are good for the more health-conscious customers. Artificial eggs and turkey bacon are great substitutions and make a great meal. Generous eight-inch pancakes are mixed from scratch, as they say. Debbie and her staff make sure the syrup is warm when it's served at the table.

Myrtle's is an award-winning diner that you will want to experience yourself.

"MAKE HUNGER THY SAUCE, AS A MEDICINE FOR HEALTH."

— Thomas Tusser

CONTACT INFO:
109 N. Broadway St.
Poplar Bluff
573-785-9203

Breakfast served all day!

CHECK NUMBER
NO. 3605140

A TRUCK STOP FAVORITE

In the small town of Sarcoxie, you will find the best country breakfast right off Interstate 44 at **The Hungry House**. Denise Reynolds opened the restaurant in 2004. Many family members are among the twenty-some employees. When travelers stop at this twenty-four-hour eatery, they love and count on good, fresh home cooking, and a lot of it. The majority of customers are truck drivers. Many of the regulars call ahead to place their orders to save time.

A new favorite on the menu is the Belly Buster. For $7.99, you get a big plate of layered biscuits, eggs, hash browns, peppers, on- ions, bacon, and sau- sage covered in gravy. They also rave about the country-fresh ham, sliced right off the bone. Apple-smoked bacon and fresh potato hash browns add to the mouth-watering menu choices.

A PERSONAL NOTE:

Denise and her staff make sure no one goes hungry. Servings will continue to be plentiful, and only fresh produce and products will do.

Denise faced a major challenge in 2008 when a care- less person's firecracker wound up under the restaurant, burning it to the ground. Denise wasn't sure she wanted to rebuild, until she read a sign placed against a concrete block near the damage: "If you re-build, they will come. We're hungry for the Hungry House." She was inspired, and building began for the opening in 2009. It has a big kitchen and storeroom, which is an improvement over the previous place.

If there's a wait, not to worry, grab one of the many rocking chairs and enjoy. The highway landmark is "good to go" now and for many years to come.

"NOTHING HELPS SCENERY LIKE HAM AND EGGS."

—Mark Twain

Guest Check

CONTACT INFO:

SERVER | TABLE | GUESTS | CHECK NUMBER

1391 Lawrence S. Outer Rd.
Sarcoxie
417-548-2604
hungryhousecafe.net

Breakfast served all day!

EATING WITH YOUR EYES

You can sleep in beauty and rise and dine to a breakfast of culinary art. Larry and Michaelene Stevens purchased the prestigious Samuel N. Dickey Mansion in 1998 to open **The Dickey House Bed and Breakfast** in Marshfield.

The Stevenses did major restoration with careful planning to accommodate the many snowbirds who travel back and forth from north and south. They also wanted to give back to the community with a place to entertain. Many dignitaries and two presidents have visited the Dickey Mansion.

All breakfasts include some form of fresh fruit or a baked apple. Breakfast choices are influenced by what fresh produce might be growing in the backyard near their two cottages. One of the signature dishes is the Breakfast Braid. The braided pastry includes thin slices of ham, eggs, bell peppers, onions, cream cheese, milk, and cheddar cheese. It's served with fruit and baked hash browns. The presentation is impressive, as you can imagine.

Larry's talent not only shows in his cooking skills, but also in his beautiful landscaping abilities and his

A PERSONAL NOTE:

Larry offers many hints for cooking, but he says for fluffier and lighter omelets, add a dash of cold water, a couple of dashes of skim milk, and a splash of corn starch. Softened cream cheese with a little milk added to any egg dish will keep it fresher longer and give it a richer flavor.

oil paintings. Larry conducts seminars and cooking classes to other potential bed-and-breakfast owners. He also organizes Murder Mystery packages that include a gourmet dinner.

The Dickey House will amuse you with its history, gorgeous antique furnishings, beautiful gardens, and their best-of-all-worlds breakfast.

CONTACT INFO:
331 S. Clay St.
Marshfield
417-468-3000
dickeyhouse.com

LIMITED BREAKFAST HOURS

BELGIAN WAFFLE AND PANCAKE HOUSE

David and Leonda Taghon are the proud owners of the **Belgian Waffle and Pancake House** in Springfield, Missouri. David's father started the restaurant in Branson when he opened the Colonial Inn. David's grandparents came over from Belgium at the start of the twentieth century and brought many family recipes. After the Springfield location opened, they opened another restaurant four years later in Ozark. Each restaurant serves about two hundred people and has an Old World décor that customers find comforting.

The waffles and pancakes dominate the menu and come in every flavor and topping that you can imagine. The featured waffle is the Pecan Waffle. The thickness and lightness of their waffles has

> ## A PERSONAL NOTE:
> The family says their secret to their amazing pancakes is that they are made with Bavarian buttermilk and a dash of real Mexican vanilla.

earned them the Best Waffle Award by *417 Magazine*. The pancakes are all from scratch, and the Blueberry Pancakes rise to the top. They contain only fresh blueberries, measure about nine inches in size, and are very light and fluffy. Of course, the usual fare of breakfast dishes are also available, like omelets and baked goods. Lunch and dinner also follow their great breakfasts.

David has taken over all the baking, and he has developed quite a reputation for his pies. Keeping up a family tradition in the food industry is a commendable feat. Sampling the breakfast that has been passed on through generations warrants a visit that you will enjoy.

Guest Check

CONTACT INFO:

SERVER   TABLE   GUESTS   CHECK NUMBER

4760 S. Campbell, Springfield

Nº 3005140

417-823-8480

1882 James River Rd., Ozark

417-582-2600

belgianwafflehouse.com

Breakfast served all day!

EAT WITH THE AMISH

The Amish community makes up 30 percent of the Mt. Vernon, Missouri, population. Their reputation for being good cooks makes it a great compliment when they eat at **The Red Barn Café**. Getting an empty seat is a challenge at this popular eating hub where everyone in town seems to meet. Shari Copenhaven, owner of three years, should be very pleased.

A PERSONAL NOTE:

The surprise bonus to this café is the bakery. Five kinds of cake, lots of cookie choices, five different freshly baked breads, and at least eleven pie options are available. Wait until you see how high the meringue toppings can get.

When you look over the menu, you will see tempting choices under the title of Plow Boy Breakfasts. I think we have a barn theme going on here. Forget having chicken-fried steak for lunch or dinner, because you can have it with three eggs for a really hearty breakfast. The eight-ounce chopped steak with three eggs is another option.

All the omelets are made with four eggs, making them quite sizable, as you can see when you order the Barnyard Omelet that is stuffed with ham, cheese, onions, and peppers. You will also get the hash browns, three silver dollar pancakes, and biscuits and gravy.

A Kid's Breakfast is pretty substantial for kids ages three to ten. For $4.25 you get one egg, two strips of bacon, and toast, or one pancake with two strips of bacon.

The cozy red-barn-painted building is nestled within a few feet from the road, so parking is a challenge. It's worth every effort, however, to get inside and taste all the fixings this place has to offer.

CONTACT INFO:
107 W. Mt. Vernon Blvd.
Mt. Vernon
417-466-4650

LIMITED BREAKFAST HOURS

A BOUTIQUE BREAKFAST

The **Walnut Street Inn Bed and Breakfast** is one of the signature businesses in Springfield. Gary and Paula Blankenship have owned this Queen Anne Victorian inn for more than ten years. They continue to build on the uniqueness that appeals to their clientele, bringing them back year after year.

Gary, the chef, loves trying new things, but his lemon-butter cream pancakes with blueberries are one of the guests' favorites. Coming in second are the individual Spinach Soufflés, which are light and airy. This is served with fresh fruit and homemade muffins. Gary is happy to accommodate his guests' individual breakfast requests.

Gary loves using Missouri-fresh products whenever he can, like the free-range chicken eggs from the nearby Millsap Farm.

A PERSONAL NOTE:

Gary said for a lighter pancake, separate your yolk from the egg white. First, beat the egg whites and then slowly fold in your yolks. If he's making omelets, he uses eggs that are room temperature and cooks them very slowly.

After breakfast, guests can gather on the inviting swing-around porch with hand-painted Corinthian columns. The guest rooms are lavishly furnished with antiques, but modern amenities are hidden to make you feel perfectly at home. Springfield has many exciting places to visit and explore, and this bed-and-breakfast has become a popular place to spend the night for many parents who visit their children at nearby Southwest State University.

Your stay here will be delightful, but it is the breakfast that "takes the cake."

CONTACT INFO:

900 E. Walnut St.

Springfield

417-864-6346

walnutstreetinn.com

LIMITED BREAKFAST HOURS

CHECK NUMBER

№ 3605140

GOOBER'S PLACE

Everything is delicious at **George's**. This restaurant was named after George Lindsey, who played Goober on the *Andy Griffith Show*. Since 1970, George and Trish Stevenson have owned this busy neighborhood eatery on the busiest street in Springfield.

Breakfast reigns here. The frequently ordered Recession Proof Breakfast gives you two eggs, hash browns, your choice of meat, and biscuits for only $2.99. Their American Fries are like no other. Fried slices of real potatoes are fried with onions, butter, and their secret seasoning, which makes them so good. They are the most popular side dish, but a plate full of these fries can also make a delicious meal all by itself. The California Omelet is a unique combination of eggs, turkey, sautéed mushrooms, broccoli, tomatoes, onions, melted Swiss cheese, and topped with slices of avocados. A variety of menu choices show up on their hot buffet as well. Mexican dishes are another feature of George's menu.

A PERSONAL NOTE:

George's prides itself on making delicious red-hot salsa. It is rich in consistency and the spicy flavor complements many of the menu choices, like their breakfast omelets. The salsa is available in a twelve-ounce jar for you to purchase and take home.

Ten seats at the counter, plus a room full of booths, are all filled with hungry patrons who visit on a regular basis.

Good recession-proof food makes George's a place to remember.

"BREAKFAST IS THE ONE MEAL AT WHICH IT IS PER-FECTLY GOOD MANNERS TO READ THE PAPER."

— Amy Vanderbilt

CONTACT INFO:
339 S. Glenstone Ave.
Springfield
417-831-6777

Breakfast served all day!

CHECK NUMBER
NO. 3605140

WHAT'S BIGGER THAN A HUBCAP?

It just takes one visit to **Billy Gail's Café** in Branson to know the answer to this question. Customers eagerly wait to get their order of paper-thin pancakes that are as big as a hubcap and hang over your plate. Ordering one of these delicious pancakes can make for a good wait, as only three pancakes will fit on the grill at one time.

Bill and Gail Blong, the owners, wanted to be very generous with all the menu choices, but it was Billy's idea to make the pancakes so big. Five pancake choices are available, but the peanut butter pancake is growing in popularity with its melted peanut butter and honey sauce. If you are not a pancake eater, you may want to try the newest breakfast entrée, the Sloppy Biscuit. French Texas toast is filled with sausage, eggs, cheese, and another slice of French toast, followed by hash browns covered in gravy.

A PERSONAL NOTE:

If you want to make a really big pancake, there are tricks to flipping it over. Gail tells her customers she flips her cakes with a red shovel from Minnesota, her home state. On a serious note, she then tells them to work around the edges, when the pancakes are done, then work to the middle, before giving them a quick flip. Yes, many are broken and don't make it to the table.

Local produce is used when at all possible. The country charm of red-checkered tablecloths and geraniums will make you feel right at home in this popular tourist spot. It's located just one mile from Missouri's top tourist attraction, Silver Dollar City. This small café was once a filling station. It is now a 1960s log cabin that only seats sixty-five people.

Everyone knows about Billy Gail's, and now you know why.

CONTACT INFO:

5291 State Hwy. 265

Branson

417-338-8883

Breakfast served all day!

A MESS TO ENJOY

The **White Grill** has been in the same location since 1938. After several owners, Jim Novack purchased this diner in 1963. Diana Wesley now runs the family-owned restaurant that involves sisters and some daughters. Diana said they keep their breakfast food simple because their regulars love the consistency of their good food that prior generations enjoyed.

Lewie Meyer, a former cook here, experimented and created what they call The Mess. Curious and hungry folks are eager to order this menu item. It's fun to watch the cooks grill fresh potato hash browns,

A PERSONAL NOTE:

These owners are not afraid to use grease and plenty of butter to make their diner food really delicious.

onions, ham, and eggs. They are combined and covered with cheese, creating quite a mess. For any meal at the White Grill, folks talk about the curly fries, called Suzy-Q's, which include the potato skins for crispiness.

The black-and-white, 1950s-diner atmosphere lends itself to the counter, where you can sit and watch all the dishes being prepared. Booths, tables, and the counter can only seat forty-five customers, so get in line. This experience is worth the wait.

"THE BREAKFAST TABLE IS NOT A BULLETIN BOARD FOR THE CURING OF HORRIBLE DREAMS AND DEPRESSING SYMPTOMS, BUT A PLACE WHERE A BRIGHT KEYNOTE FOR THE DAY IS STRUCK."

—Prof. B.G. Jeffries, MD

Guest Check

CONTACT INFO:

SERVER	TABLE	GUESTS	CHECK NUMBER

NO. 3605140

200 N. Commercial St.

Nevada

417-667-9388

Breakfast served all day!

UNDER TEN OR OVER SIXTY

Freda Crates knows the value of an affordable meal, especially when you are under ten or over sixty. Her special bargain choices for these folks are listed separately—like one pancake for $1.25. If you just want biscuits and gravy, it's only $1.10. How about one egg, one meat, and one pancake for just $3.75? Marshfield, Missouri, is where you can find this unique café called **Freda's Uptown Café**. The uptown location brings in 270 folks a day, and on Saturday she can sometimes serve as many as 315.

The Uptown Omelet is a popular favorite that includes three eggs, ham, bacon, onions, cheese, bell peppers, and mushrooms for $6.35. Everyone loves Freda's biscuits. They accompany each order for a very good reason. After they are freshly baked, the biscuits are buttered and put on the grill, which creates a toastier bite of flavor.

A PERSONAL NOTE:
Freda's heart says she needs to give back to the community for her success. Sometimes it is just a free breakfast for someone who is down on his luck. When some young boys needed to make money, she bought them a lawn mower to get lawn jobs. Her slogan is, "We're here to feed, not fatten anyone!"

Freda used to be a waitress at this café until four years ago when she became the owner. She and her employees enjoy the café and the customers, whom they seem to know by name. The love shows in the food as well.

"MODERATION; SMALL HELPINGS. SAMPLE A LITTLE BIT OF EVERYTHING. THESE ARE THE SECRETS OF HAPPINESS AND GOOD HEALTH."

—Julia Child

Guest Check

CONTACT INFO:

CHECK NUMBER
N° 3605140

210 W. Jackson St.
Marshfield
417-859-7251

Breakfast served all day!

AUNT MARTHA'S PANCAKE HOUSE

A Springfield landmark when it comes to breakfast and brunch is **Aunt Martha's Pancake House**. Martha Hayworth, known professionally as "Aunt Martha" as a member of the Ozark Jubilee, decided to open this full-service restaurant in the heart of the fast-growing town. There is no question that the main menu item here is pancakes, made with Martha's secret recipe.

In 1964, Swede and Ruth Freeman purchased the business after Martha's health began to fail. Ruth continued to run the restaurant until her daughter, Brenda, took over in 2001.

A PERSONAL NOTE:

Brenda is now the only person who knows the secret in making up the dry ingredients for their pancakes and waffles. All the syrups are made fresh and are thinner than most, and come in many flavors.

The pancake house has seen many a country western musician who has passed through this busy tourist region. Willie Nelson makes frequent stops here and brags about when he used to wash dishes at the restaurant in 1960. He claims he always has a job open if his career fizzles. Willard Scott from *The Today Show* has also made an appearance.

Pancakes, waffles, and an entire breakfast menu will tempt you, but when you experience one of the pancake favorites, you will never forget it. The Chocolate Pancake is a rich chocolate nugget in cocoa batter. The end result

is a light, plate-sized chocolate pancake served with a large scoop of vanilla ice cream in the center. Chocolate syrup is then lightly swirled over the top. The idea for such a pancake came from a seven-year-old customer's request. It continues to be the sweet-tooth choice of many who do not see this combination very often.

The quaint, one-room eatery is lined with Martha's and Ruth's memorabilia collected through the years, which is a conversation tool for many a visitor. You need to see and eat for yourself.

CONTACT INFO:
1700 E. Cherokee St.
Springfield
417-881-3505
auntmarthaspancakehouse.com

Breakfast served all day!

WHAT'S GREAT AT THE LAKE?

Tourists and locals alike love the **On the Rise Bakery and Wood-Fired Bistro** at the Lake of the Ozarks in Osage. Mike and Cheryl Castle bought the bakery in 1995, but it is Mike's long history of flipping food at different restaurants at the lake that makes him a pro. His Culinary Institute of America diploma prepared him for the success he now enjoys.

Breakfast shines here because of the many creative choices as well as the freshly baked breads and pastries. Lunch is also served.

Whoever heard of eggs Benedict choices like the Oscar, which includes lump blue crab meat and white asparagus? The Californian adds roasted turkey, artichoke hearts, Roma tomatoes, and caramelized onions. Their manager's favorite is the European, which uses raw spinach and caramelized onions, topped with pancetta and Parmesan. For a mouth-watering combination, try the Bananas Foster French Toast. Bananas embellish the toast with warm caramelized syrup.

A PERSONAL NOTE:

For an extra splash of flavor in making Bananas Foster syrup, add a little orange juice. To make a lavender flavor, boil lavender sprigs to get an oil that mixes well with other ingredients.

It's no wonder *Southern Living* magazine listed On the Rise in their top-ten restaurants.

"BREAKFAST APPOINT-MENTS CREATE SALES OP-PORTUNITIES. CLIENTS TEND TO BE FRESH AND MORE RECEPTIVE THEN."

— Byrd Baggett

Guest Check

CONTACT INFO:

5439 Hwy. 54

Osage Beach

573-348-4224

ontherisebakery.com

CHECK NUMBER
NO. 3605140

Breakfast served all day!

SHOP, SIP, AND DINE

When you walk into the **You Say Tomato** grocery and café, you see all the homegrown goodness of Missouri. Fresh and packaged products come from places like Good Acres Farm. The café in Kansas City, Missouri, combines this goodness with the finished product of delicious eats.

Mark Wingard and Randy Parks, owners of four years, named the restaurant and grocery from a lyric in the song "Let's Call the Whole Thing Off. "The title is fitting for the theme of produce and freshly made menu selections. In business since 1948, the restaurant/ deli later added some groceries to sell. Mark and Randy also employ folks who actually live in the neighborhood.

When you place your breakfast order at the counter, the choices are plentiful. The seating capacity is forty-five, if you choose to sit instead of go.

A PERSONAL NOTE:

Mark and Randy harvest their fresh herbs right outside their door where they grow them with all the tall, mixed grasses and flowers.

The Quiche of the Day is notable and the popular choice can be ordered all day. The crust is freshly made with real butter instead of lard. It makes a flakier crust and is more appealing to vegetarians. Healthier choices are no problem here. How about a Honey Vanilla Bean Yogurt with Berries. Muffins, which vary by season, are a great companion to this and other breakfast choices.

An extended coffee and beverage menu are an attraction to many who frequent this café on a regular basis. Sunday brunches are not to be missed because of the variety of unique dishes that include all of their quiches.

"TASTES ARE MADE, NOT BORN."

—Mark Twain

Guest Check

CONTACT INFO:
2801 Holmes St.
Kansas City
816-756-5097
ystkc.com

CHECK NUMBER
№ 3605140

LIMITED BREAKFAST HOURS

ANIMAL LOVER'S GETAWAY

Lois Hoover loves animals. It shows in her "Adopt a Pet" participation and her business, the **Su Casa Bed and Breakfast** in Kansas City.

Her ranch-style home and five-acre outdoor area are covered with American West and Native American artwork. You can enjoy your breakfast as you laze around the large in-ground pool and watch the grazing animals that include llamas, goats, horses, ducks, and geese. If you want to hang out indoors, a twenty-seat theater and game room await you.

A breakfast bar is available when you wake in the morning, but because of Lois's experience as a bed-and-breakfast chef for twelve years, she will amaze you with her breakfast entrées. She likes to mix things up by always trying new recipes.

The Pecan Croissant French Toast is a mouth-watering combination of sliced croissants dipped in batter that includes eggs, grated orange peel, fresh orange juice, and cinnamon. It's then drizzled with butter and pecans before

A PERSONAL NOTE:

Lois will make a point to ask you about any dietary conditions before you visit, as most bed-and-breakfasts do, but she takes it a step further by asking what you enjoy most for breakfast, rather than following a regularly planned menu. She also makes a point to tell you they are pet- and children-friendly, which is unique.

baking. The final touch is a dash of powdered sugar before serving with warm syrup.

When Lois arranges a romantic weekend for a couple, she loves making her chocolate-covered strawberries extra special by cutting out the core and stuffing them with mascarpone (Italian cream cheese) and brown sugar.

The extra touch makes breakfast one of the best amenities at this clever bed-and-breakfast.

Guest Check

CONTACT INFO:
9004 E. 92nd St.
Kansas City
816-965-5647
sucasabb.com

CHECK NUMBER
N°. 3605140

LIMITED BREAKFAST HOURS

BACKROAD FOOD

You don't have to take the back roads to get to the **Backroads Grill** in Blackwater. It's located right in the heart of Main Street before you cross the bridge over the Missouri River. There's no question this place is well known by the locals, but its location also captures the tourists who frequent this small, historic town that feels like a movie set. Blackwater was named after the Blackwater Creek that runs through it.

Caitlynd Weekley and her husband, Bryan, have only owned the diner for three years. They both are young trained chefs who are using their creative juices not only in the restaurant business, but also in the Iron Horse Hotel, which they lease across the street. They serve dinner at the hotel on a limited basis.

The diner serves three meals a day, but breakfast is the highlight, with their customized omelets and pancakes that are the size of a dinner plate. The three-egg omelet with hash browns and toast is the most frequently ordered breakfast item. Breakfast sandwiches are generous and very affordable. There are delicious combinations to choose from, and nothing costs more than $3.50.

As you munch away, you will get a kick out of seeing the local folks featured in photos along the wall. The back

> **A PERSONAL NOTE:**
> Caitlynd feels it's important for her help to get to know what their customers like and how they like it. This encourages repeat customers.

of the menu says it best: "Good Food at the Crossroads of Somewhere and No Where!" After you visit, you'll remember where.

"OUR LIVES ARE NOT IN THE LAP OF THE GODS, BUT IN THE LAP OF OUR COOKS."

— Lin Yutang

CONTACT INFO:

106 Main St.
Blackwater
660-846-2220

CHECK NUMBER
№ 3605140

Breakfast served all day!

THE BIG GREEK BREAKFAST

Tina Alyea opened the **Missouri Mud Company Greek Deli and Coffee House** eleven years ago and hasn't looked back since. In the spirit of her Greek ancestors, she includes her daughter, sisters, and anyone else in the family who loves to cook and enjoys people. Just like the popular movie *My Big Fat Greek Wedding,* her family lives close together.

As expected, the breakfast and lunch menus have a Greek influence, like George's Greek Omelet that has four eggs, feta cheese, tomatoes, onions, and their special Greek spices. You can add gyro meat, and it's served with pita bread. If you want a stuffed breakfast pita, you can pick your choice of ingredients. The deli makes all their bread, which includes their famous and delicious Cappuccino Fudge Muffins. Their many sandwich choices include a variety of bread options.

A PERSONAL NOTE:

Tina and her family are big garlic users. They make their own combination of spices that goes in everything from salads to omelets. She says most people cook too blandly. She says you should double all your spices, except salt, when cooking.

All the produce for the restaurant comes from the many family gardens, including apples and figs from their dad's garden.

Whether you are just having a coffee, a homemade bagel, omelets, or a plate full of biscuits and gravy, you will be experiencing a big, delicious Greek breakfast served with love and a lot of family attention.

Guest Check

CONTACT INFO:
1294 W. Foxwood Dr.
Raymore
816-322-6262
missourimud.net

CHECK NUMBER
NO. 3605140

LIMITED BREAKFAST HOURS

WHAT'S IN THE ROOM?

In 1994, Ted Hubiger and Andy Sloan of Kansas City, Missouri, met at a brewpub not realizing they would someday be the co-owners of **Room 39**. The awards followed their fine reputation for good food, especially their breakfasts. The cast of the Walt Bodine Show of Kansas City said it was the best breakfast they have had anywhere. Room 39's quiche was recognized in the Best of KC Awards.

The Room's very clever, unique, and attractive breakfast item is their Oven Eggs. This is prepared by cutting off the top of a hamburger bun, hollowing the center out for an egg, and topping it with Genoa salami and gruyère cheese before cooking it in the oven. It's served with fruit salad on the side. Elegant choices like the Smoked Salmon Scramble offer house-cured and smoked salmon with cream cheese, scallions, and soft scrambled eggs. This comes with breakfast potatoes and toast. The Brioche French Toast with bacon is another gourmet delight made with cinnamon egg custard.

A PERSONAL NOTE:

They make their popular Brioche French Toast in a cylindrical pan. The chef rolls out the homemade combination and cuts in one-inch slices for extra goodness.

Twelve different farmers, plus their own father, supply them with fresh Missouri produce, which includes many herbs.

Their coffee is made from Arabica beans from Ethiopia and Costa Rica but roasted by the local Broadway Roasting Company. The Danesi espresso is imported from Italy. They like the creaminess and lack of bitterness. Every drink is made by skilled baristas.

The midtown Kansas City location was their first restaurant, followed by the Leawood, Kansas, location. Room 39 is well worth the find.

Guest Check

CONTACT INFO:
1719 W. 39th St.
Kansas City
816-753-3939

rm39.com

LIMITED BREAKFAST HOURS

CHECK NUMBER
N° 3605140

AN IRISH BREAKFAST

There's more than a good Irish breakfast at the **Hatchery House Bed and Breakfast**. Jan and Larry Jabara purchased the B&B over two years ago and moved into the second floor of the 1845 Federal-style home.

You'll find this gem just one block off Main Street in the heart of historic Weston, Missouri. Across the street is the popular Weston Brewing Company and O'Malley's Pub. The historic pub is located sixty feet underground, where many a bottle of liquor has been stored. The Irish music and atmosphere will enhance your Irish experience when visiting the Hatchery House.

Jan's breakfast speciality is her Irish Pie. It combines all the main food groups into a delicious casserole. She likes to find out her guests' preferences ahead of time, but folks know they are in for a touch of Ireland regardless of the ingredients Jan uses. Homemade cookies give the rooms a wonderful aroma each day, as Jan rotates from sugar cookies to shortbread. Custom-blended coffees are available as well.

The Vaughn Orchards and the Western Red Barn Farm, located nearby, are handy for all the fresh produce

A PERSONAL NOTE:

The B&B was named the Hatchery House because in the earlier years it had become a boarding house for many families. These families had many babies. Thus, it was known as the baby hatchery, and now you know the rest of the story.

the B&B uses. Jan and Larry also encourage their guests to visit the farms.

When five o'clock rolls around on weekends, you will find a wine tasting promoting the nearby Pirtle Winery.

The Jabaras include the whole community in their business, making sure visitors do not miss all the attractions Weston has to offer. This kind of hospitality will no doubt result in spending more days at the Hatchery House.

Guest Check

CONTACT INFO:

CHECK NUMBER

№ 3605140

618 Short St.
Weston
816-640-5700
hatcherybb.com

LIMITED BREAKFAST HOURS

EAT AMONG FRIENDS

Many friends meet up at **Ginger Sue's**, on the historic square in Liberty, Missouri. David Bradley and his wife, Ginger Sue Fuller, opened this clever café in 2006. They offer a full and creative menu for breakfast.

Specialty coffees and five kinds of smoothies are a highlight to start your day, but it's the breakfast offerings that keep folks coming back. Omelets are a big deal because they are offered in many unusual combinations like the Aloha Awakea, which has the taste of a Maui sunrise, with a mix of pineapple, ham, and cheddar jack cheeses, topped with coconut. A Don't Be Crabby Omelet is a medley of green onion and cheddar with crabmeat. To get a taste of the West Coast, try the omelet made with seasoned bacon, sliced avocado, and shredded cheddar cheese, topped with salsa and sour cream. For a more sophisticated dish, you may want to try the Crab Benedict. Crab and Andouille sausage are served atop a honey-wheat English muffin with over-easy eggs, sliced green onion, and hollandaise sauce. Their breakfast potatoes are served on the side. French toast, waffles, and buttermilk pancakes are also favorites.

A PERSONAL NOTE:

Ginger feels the best-kept secret of her café is their seasoned bacon. It's covered with rosemary, sugar, and pepper before its baked good and crispy.

A stop at Ginger Sue's is a happy and satisfying way to start your day. The youthful ownership brings energy and creativity to this town of 30,000 folks. Liberty is also the home to William Jewel College. As the café says on their menu, "Come eat among friends!"

"DINING WITH ONE'S FRIENDS AND BELOVED FAMILY IS CERTAINLY ONE OF LIFE'S PRIMAL AND MOST INNOCENT DELIGHTS, ONE THAT IS BOTH SOUL SATISFYING AND ETERNAL."

— Julia Child

Guest Check

CONTACT INFO:

CHECK NUMBER

Nº 3605140

12 W. Kansas St.

Liberty

816-407-7707

gingersues.com

Breakfast served all day!

BIG BISCUITS

The four-by-two-inch biscuits are big and delicious at the **Big Biscuit** restaurant in Independence, Missouri. It is the signature food item that most folks order, with homemade sausage gravy that you can order in small or large proportions. Dan Gerson opened their first location eleven years ago, and they have been feeding many hungry folks ever since.

The menu features a BIG choice in the scramblers, pancakes, waffles, and even some BIG healthy breakfast choices. A Country Benedict is a load of scrambled eggs served on a split biscuit and sausage patty and covered with sausage gravy. The dish is served with a side of potatoes. The Workout Scrambler is egg substitute scrambled with spinach and mushrooms. It's served with fruit and

A PERSONAL NOTE:

Their biscuits are baked all day long, ensuring that they are always hot and fresh. The staff brings more than 650 biscuits to their customers each day.

raisin toast. For an indulging choice, the Caramel Berry Bliss French Toast is thickly cut and topped with caramel sauce, powdered sugar, strawberries, and blueberries.

Two other locations in Blue Springs and Shawnee, Kansas, also serve the big biscuits in a big way.

"I WENT TO A RESTAURANT THAT SERVES 'BREAKFAST AT ANYTIME,' SO I ORDERED FRENCH TOAST DURING THE RENAISSANCE."

—Steven Wright

CONTACT INFO:

16506 E. Hwy. 40, Independence
816-478-6958
and
530 N. Hwy. 7, Blue Springs
816-229-3108
bigbiscuitrestaurant.com

Breakfast served all day!

A DIAMOND IN THE ROUGH

Willie Diggs has a restaurant history that has taken him to California, Florida, Kansas City, St. Joseph, and now to his hometown of Barnard, Missouri. Barnard is where his grandfather and father operated a general store in the 1940s and 1950s.

Just barely settled, Willie is trying to make his own mark with good, fresh homemade cooking that he knows the locals and tourists alike will love.

The **Barnard Roadhouse Grill** can seat seventy folks. Come breakfast time, you better get there early, because only so many biscuits and gravy are made each day. When they are gone, they are gone. The biscuits are "Southern style" to Willie. They are bigger than your normal biscuit, and the recipe has been handed down through three generations.

A PERSONAL NOTE:

Willie's family has generations of meat cutters. They make their own breakfast sausage using their own secret spices. They grind pork shoulders and make their own patties. For their hamburger meat, they take the high-quality bottom round, top round, and chuck roast and grind them together on a daily basis to keep up with demand.

The Farmer's Breakfast is a hearty platter of three eggs, hash browns, two sausage patties, three slices of bacon, biscuits, gravy, and toast for $8.95. A new item Willie is introducing is called the Haystack. Items are stacked, starting with a large sliced biscuit, gravy, two eggs, and topped with fresh-cut hash browns to give it a haystack look. You will also want to try Willie's place for the best hamburger around. Word spreads fast about quality eating places, so you may have already heard there is a big surprise in the small town of Barnard.

CONTACT INFO:

421 4th St.

CHECK NUMBER

No̱ 3605140

Barnard

660-652-4040

barnardroadhouse.wordpress.com

Breakfast served all day!

WHO'S IN THE KITCHEN?

You will find **Kate's Kitchen** in Gladstone, Missouri, near Kansas City. The staff are friendly, and delicious offerings are plentiful, but if you are lucky, you will be greeted by Kate herself.

Kate, the six-year-old daughter of co-owner Dave Henerex, occasionally greets customers who come to this small, super friendly place to enjoy breakfast. Her five-year-old brother, Ronnie, has been known to be her partner in crime. Joey Franke, the other co-owner, said how proud they are of their two-year-old establishment that found a quick following.

A PERSONAL NOTE:

The cooks always make food fresh to order. They are quick to tell you they can cook healthy and still make a great breakfast.

Some of the menu items have been named after customers, like Ken's Cadillac Breakfast Burrito Scrambler. Ken, who drives a Cadillac, arrives daily when the restaurant opens. The Stuffed French Toast is one of their more unusual menu delights. Sausage, melted cheese, and scrambled eggs rest between two pieces of French toast.

A welcome surprise here is the large selection of healthy breakfast choices called their Fitness Corner. The Breakfast Banana Split has yogurt, granola, and fresh berries, surrounded by a banana and dusted with powdered sugar. It's served with the muffin of the day for just $5.50. The Benedict choices on English muffins have homemade

hollandaise sauce. They can sport a crab cake with tomato or a slice of turkey with avocado.

This is a place where the owners are happy to sit a
spell with you, and if you're lucky, you may get to say
hello to Kate.

CONTACT INFO:
8002 N. Oak Trafficway
Gladstone
816-436-7200
kateskitchenkc.com

Breakfast served all day!

A CLASSY BREAKFAST

A real must see and taste in Kansas City is the **Classic Cup Café**, located in the Country Club Plaza. This plaza is known for its upscale shopping and beautiful fountains. Kansas City is known as the City of Fountains. This European-style bistro opened in 1990 offering full dining services, but breakfast is outstanding and the menu is quite extensive.

The daily menu for breakfast is always offered, but the Sunday brunch is an opportunity to sample many of their creative dishes. You might want to try Mama's Buttermilk Pancakes with smoked bacon and maple syrup. Oven Baked Dutch Puffed Pancakes comes with fresh fruit. Florentine Ham Frittata is layers of spinach, ham, pasta, and cheese that will melt in your mouth. The Pacific Northwest Benedict features smoked salmon, or you may want to order an omelet your way. The pastries are all baked in-house, and the many sides are a show by themselves.

> **A PERSONAL NOTE:**
>
> The café has its own gourmet buttermilk pancake mix for sale. They use 1 percent low-fat buttermilk. One 27.8-ounce bag makes forty pancakes for only $3.50. You need to email pancake@classiccup.com to order.

The inside classy décor is to be admired, but the real show is the outdoor seating area that outlines the corner café. The people-watching and the scenic architecture of the plaza are all candy for the eyes.

The awards continue to mount for this café. They were awarded Ingram's Silver Ladle for Best Restaurant. For ten years in a row, they have won the Plaza Art Fair's Best Food Award. They continue to be listed in the top ten of Best Kansas City Restaurants.

You too will be a winner when you enjoy your breakfast at the Classic Cup Café.

Guest Check

CONTACT INFO:

CHECK NUMBER

No. 3605140

301 W. 47th St.
Kansas City
816-753-1840
classiccup.com

Breakfast served all day!

A FIREMAN'S DREAM

In 2008, Bill and Brenda Crow opened the **Cook Shack Café** in Kansas City. Bill, a retired fireman, had a dream of owning his own kitchen, as he was the cook for his firehouse for twenty-nine years. The "cook shack" was a term he took from his tenure at the fire station.

The café has more than good food to brag about. The locals love it so much the *Wednesday Shopper* voted the café No. 3 for best waitresses. Family members work here as well, and they all take pride in not cutting corners for their customers. Bill said he and his family have fond memories of this place, as they would go here to get treats many years ago when they were young.

The tiny establishment only has eight tables, plus the counter seating, so it's no wonder folks can wait forty-five minutes or more.

Combinations like the Hamburger Omelet and the Tenderloin Omelet get a lot of attention, as do their homemade biscuits and gravy.

The Crows try to support local food vendors by buying their eggs from a nearby Amish farm. Good word of mouth and the local support of the police and fire departments boost the energy and success of this popular

A PERSONAL NOTE:

The staff feels their omelets are better because they sauté their ingredients before going into the omelet mix. They put it all on the grill, spray with water, then cover with a lid to steam.

neighborhood restaurant. Go see for yourself what the "fire" is all about.

CONTACT INFO:
8050 Wornall
Kansas City
816-333-0013
cookshackcafellc.com

Breakfast served all day!

HOME AWAY FROM HOME

Just ask the locals in Riverside, Liberty, or Independence where they want to have breakfast, and the most popular answer will be the **Corner Café**.

In 1983, Ed and Kathie Rule helped the future of Riverside, Missouri, with their fast-growing forty-seat restaurant. In 1985, a fire broke out and destroyed a warehouse next to their eatery. They salvaged many treasures, many family heirlooms, and opened the new Corner Café in 1994.

When you walk in the entrance of the café, you are greeted with heavenly smells of fresh-baked rolls and bread. You are not disappointed when you sit down to see their breakfast choices on the menu.

A PERSONAL NOTE:
The Rules believe that excellent food and service make everyone feel like they are part of the family.

The Corner Special is a favorite, which includes two of their buttermilk pancakes, eggs, and your choice of meat. For an omelet with a "kick," order the Gringo. The eggs contain chorizo sausage, pepper jack cheese, hash browns, sweet peppers, and onions, topped with green onions, salsa, and sour cream. The lighter side of the menu has eight healthy choices and smaller proportions.

Did I mention they've been honored for the best biscuits and gravy in local contests?

I say take advantage of this hometown restaurant that

loves serving you a fresh breakfast right from the oven and grill.

> ## "I DON'T HAVE A PROBLEM WITH CAFFEINE; I HAVE A PROBLEM WITHOUT IT."
>
> —Unknown

Guest Check

CONTACT INFO:

4541 N.W. Gateway Ave., Riverside
816-741-2570

N⁰ 3605140

8301 N. Flintlock Rd., Liberty
816-415-0050

4215 S. Little Blue Pkwy., Independence
816-350-7000
www.thecornercafe.com

Breakfast served all day!

GRAB AND GO IN K.C.

Steven Hyatt worked for the previous owner of **The Silver Spoon** in downtown Kansas City before he and Steven Nelson purchased the restaurant five years ago. Catering to the business community and convention goers, the café's appetizing menu and quick service make it a big success. After you place your order at the counter, you can enjoy the street activity and sidewalk view as you munch your breakfast.

Many customers brag about their customized Breakfast Burritos. These are loaded with all your favorites at your request. The Southwest Casserole is a standard favorite and large enough to satisfy any appetite. The base is fried cubed potatoes, green peppers, onions, eggs, cheese, and your choice of meat. The homemade picante sauce is made with an extra-spicy kick, and it makes a great condiment for the casserole. You might choose the salsa with shredded cheese for another kick. Their bread choices come from a local bakery, and are an attraction in themselves.

A PERSONAL NOTE:
Steven Hyatt's wife Christina has made a successful and delicious contribution to the business. She bakes cookies that attract all ages. Chocolate chip are the favorites of course, but the iced sugar cookies are a big hit, especially during the holidays.

It's nice to know where to get a good breakfast in not a lot of time and for not a lot of money. The eighty seats inside are taken by folks who know your name—or will before you go. The café will likely know what you want and how you like it.

"TO EAT WELL IN ENGLAND, YOU SHOULD HAVE BREAKFAST 3 TIMES A DAY."
— W. Somerset Maugham

Guest Check

CONTACT INFO:
120 W. 12th St.
Kansas City
816-221-9998
thesilverspooncafe.com

LIMITED BREAKFAST HOURS

CHECK NUMBER
N⁰ 3605140

FIVE-CENT COFFEE

Believe it or not, in the twenty-first century you can still get a cup of coffee for five cents at the **Vandalia Drug** in Vandalia.

It gets better. In 1953, John P. Fitzgerald, the original owner, said he would never raise the price of a cup of coffee. This was his way of expressing his gratitude for the loyal business the locals had provided him through the years. Several times a week you are likely to get a FREE cup of coffee because of the generosity of those who want to celebrate an event or remember someone special. They call it "coffee for the house." Patrons tell Joe Salios, the current owner and pharmacist of fifteen years, that they want to sponsor coffee on a certain day. They leave a ten dollar deposit and settle up at later.

Volunteers like John Fitzgerald and others gladly help brew coffee, wipe tables, and greet the daily customers.

Seating is precious with just nine spaces at the counter and a couple of booths. Ten years ago, it was time to replace the tattered stools; so for a one-hundred-dollar contribution, you got your name put on a new stool. This is a big deal if you want a place to sit, but standing room is common and perfectly acceptable.

The closest thing to having a breakfast here is a donut

from the local IGA store. The drug store does not have a full kitchen, so many choose to eat at the local Dairy Queen down the street.

This morning coffee gathering is a "Main Street USA" experience, and you can't beat the price.

CONTACT INFO:

112 N. Main St.

Vandalia

573-594-2136

COFFEE ALL DAY

BEER FOR BREAKFAST?

Yes, a world-famous root beer is a popular choice ordered with breakfast at the **Mark Twain Dinette and Family Restaurant** in Hannibal.

Most folks who pay a visit to Hannibal are counting on a great historic tour of Mark Twain's home along the riverbank. They are never disappointed, as Hannibal has become one of the choice destinations in Missouri travel.

They will likewise discover this historic dinette that opened in 1942. Marion Pennello, its original owner, is still believed to haunt the restaurant, misplacing objects and turning off lights. John and Kay Bogue are the current owners, and they brag about their reputation to many tourists by saying, "This is the place where all the locals eat."

A PERSONAL NOTE: There are two to four batches of root beer normally made in one week. During the summer, when making all those root beer floats, they can go through a week's worth in one day.

A great breakfast menu offers the popular 2 Eggs, 2 Meats, 2 Pancakes, or the Lumberjack for the bigger appetite, which includes three buttermilk pancakes, two eggs, and your choice of meat. The restaurant's signature product is home-brewed root beer. It's a two-day process. They dissolve the sugar water and then make the mixture of the sassafras root and other ingredients in a big vat. It then it goes to a tank where it's ready for serving. They serve more root beer than any other soda. It is even more preferred than coffee with their breakfast orders.

You are likely to find bus tours at this friendly breakfast destination, as it can seat 165 folks.

Employee Scott Houser started working at the dinette as a curb server in 1987 and is now the manager. Vicki Anderson has been a waitress here for forty-four years. They know locals by name and will soon know yours when you visit.

> **"I MUST HAVE A DRINK OF BREAKFAST."**
>
> — W. C. Fields

Guest Check

CONTACT INFO:

CHECK NUMBER

N° 3605140

400 N. Third St.

Hannibal

573-221-5300

marktwaindinette.com

LIMITED BREAKFAST HOURS

A TASTE OF ROCHEPORT

The Lewis and Clark Expedition passed near Rocheport, Missouri, on June 7, 1804, and ate breakfast at the mouth of a large creek called the Big Manitou.

The charming town is the location of another great breakfast that is served at the **Yates House Bed and Breakfast** in the heart of Rocheport. In 1983, Conrad and Dixie Yates started their B&B, which was just open on weekends until 1999 when they restored the Garden House next door. A commercial kitchen was added in 2003 with a focus on fine dining. By this time, they both were full-time innkeepers.

Breakfast became the highlight of their guests' visit. The breakfast choices are expansive and enticing. You can read all about each one in their cookbook available for purchase.

A PERSONAL NOTE:

When you make hollandaise sauce, bring your water to boil, turn off, and then put your bowl over the hot water before preparing your sauce.

The Crème Brule French Toast is most frequently made. Heavy cream, large eggs, sugar, and a vanilla bean are processed before pouring over challah bread. The nice bite-size pieces are served with real maple syrup and fresh fruit.

The Yateses are pleased to be able to purchase fresh produce from local farmers who can provide fresh goat cheese and free-range chicken eggs. Rest assured that each additional night you stay the menu will change to include items like pumpkin pancakes and sautéed apples.

Foodie groups, consisting mostly of couples, can arrange a dinner component to their stay by participating in the dinner preparations. They also visit the Les Bourgeois Winery nearby to choose their wine for the dinner. When the dinner is finished, they are served by Conrad and Dixie.

The Yates House B&B is fortunate to have the Katy Trail right in their backyard and specialty shops on the connecting streets. You do, indeed, get a good taste of Rocheport.

Guest Check

CONTACT INFO:

CHECK NUMBER

N⁰ 3605140

305 Second St.
Rocheport
573-698-2129
yateshouse.com

LIMITED BREAKFAST HOURS

A CITY OF ITS OWN

Pancake City serves a vital business in Kirksville, Missouri, in more ways than one. If you attend or want to visit Truman State University or A.T. Still University-Kirksville College of Osteopathic Medicine, you can bet on having a great breakfast a time or two at this popular restaurant that opened in 1983.

A PERSONAL NOTE:

Pancake City employs students from all the local schools. They spend many hours there. If they are not working, they are studying.

A multitude of choices are available for breakfast, especially if you have pancakes on your mind. The Potato Pancake Platter is served with two eggs, bacon or sausage, and toast. Pancakes come by the stack or by the platter. Your choices are strawberry, blueberry, apple cinnamon, pecan, chocolate chip, peanut butter, Reese's Peanut Butter Cup, cherry, and Georgia peach.

It's not all about pancakes, because they have their own version of the slinger. It's called the Nova Slinger, and features a quarter-pound black Angus cheeseburger. French toast, waffles, and omelets will also tempt you.

Charles and Cindy Lewellen, the owners, said that many of their employees have been with them for many years and take pride in the service they offer. The restaurant's success goes twenty-four hours a day, except Sunday and Monday. That takes dedication.

CONTACT INFO:
2102 N. Baltimore St.
Kirksville
660-665-6002
pancakecitykirksville.com

Breakfast served all day!

DRIVE, SLEEP, AND DINE

If you are traveling near Trenton Lake in Trenton, you may want to visit **Lakeview Motor Lodge**. If you spend the night in their forty-six-bed motel, or are just passing by, you will discover a delicious breakfast waiting for you in their restaurant/coffee shop.

Ian and Ali Gray are sixteen years into their business and are pleased that the locals are happy and hang out on a daily basis. Breakfast choices are always available, but their breakfast buffet is the "big enchilada," as they say.

The casseroles are all homemade, like the Baked French Toast that starts with a bottom layer of caramelized pecans, Texas toast, and covered with a custard sauce that blends it all together. Jake's Corned Beef Hash Casserole is another popular favorite, and rarely seen in restaurants. He named it Veatch after his deceased grandmother, who gave him the recipe. The casserole can change in content, but the bacon and sausage combo is memorable. Ali, who is English, brags about her homemade hollandaise sauce for her Eggs Benedict.

> **A PERSONAL NOTE:**
>
> They add puréed bananas to all the muffin mixes to make them moister.

Their dedication to the local clientele is demonstrated by supporting the local farmers like Mitchell Meats in nearby Chillicothe, Missouri. The restaurant's rustic décor displays artwork from local artists, which includes beautiful stained glass pieces made by one of the employees.

When you get to Trenton and ask folks where you can get a good breakfast, Lakeview is their first recommendation.

"ALL HAPPINESS DEPENDS ON A LEISURELY BREAKFAST."

— John Gunther

Guest Check

CONTACT INFO:
3307 E. Tenth St.

CHECK NUMBER
№ 3605140

Trenton
660-359-2235

Breakfast served all day!

IT TAKES TWO

When you visit the **Trump Heritage Haus Bed and Breakfast** in Kahoka, you get to experience the hospitality of two owners who happen to be sisters-in-law. In 2006, Marvis and Carol Trump turned the family home into a bed-and-breakfast on their one hundred acres. Carol's husband farms the rest of the property. After the death of Marvis's parents, the family decided not to sell the farm and let the third generation occupy the house.

All the bedrooms are named after the early ladies of the house. The grand estate was built in 1875, has an open staircase, leaded and beveled doors, and a wide array of antiques. There is more than one dining room where you can enjoy your breakfast. The rooms are also used for entertaining groups for special occasions. Carol and Marvis enjoy all the themed events where they can decorate and provide creative food.

The sisters-in-law each bring their own recipes to the table. Marvis loves making her egg casserole for breakfast. It starts with crust-less bread, ham, American cheese, and more bread, before adding the egg mixture. Crushed potato chips and melted butter top it off. This is refrigerated overnight, so it's ready for baking the next morning. Carol prefers her French Toast Casserole. The bread is soaked overnight with eggs, cinnamon, and milk. Warm

A PERSONAL NOTE:

No substitutes. Marvis believes in using real food, like real butter, olive oil, half-and-half, and fresh, homemade bread for all your dishes.

maple syrup with pecans is the perfect topping.

Menus change daily and are certainly altered to the guests' diet and preference. I say double your pleasure when you visit this guesthouse.

"IF YOU'RE AFRAID TO USE BUTTER, USE CREAM."

— Julia Child

CONTACT INFO:

E. Main St.

Kahoka

660-341-5650 or 660-341-8002

trumpheritagehaus.com

CHECK NUMBER

№ 3605140

LIMITED BREAKFAST HOURS

BIG IS BETTER

The **Pioneer Café** in Marshall won Rural Missouri's Best Dessert in the Northeast Region of the state, and you would all agree if you had a taste of their delicious breakfast dessert. The talk of the town is their ten-inch cinnamon bun that fills an entire dinner plate. The thickness of the bun is impressive, but the icing takes the cake. The buttery white icing is made with a lot of love, and it is drizzled heavily around the plate. This BIG delight has a very little price of $1.99.

Carol Adams, the owner, said the café has been in the family for twenty-eight years. It is the location of the former Valle Drive Inn that everyone in town grew up with. Some of the locals still call it by that name, but Carol doesn't mind because of the fond memories.

A PERSONAL NOTE:

Carol uses cream cheese when she makes her icing for the cinnamon rolls. Powdered sugar, butter, and dash of vanilla are the main ingredients.

The local "boys," as Carol calls them, frequent the café daily. They share the local news, politics, and, of course, gossip. One gentleman picks up a friend who is blind and brings him daily to share the companionship. The fellas love the daily special of two eggs, two pancakes, and choice of meat. The other favorite option is their Texas French Toast. Carol only uses family recipes. She brags about their reputation for homemade pies. Customers not only buy it by the slice, but they also can buy the whole pie for just under ten dollars.

The great food and the friendly atmosphere of the local folks are a good reason to visit, but if you have a sweet tooth, the cinnamon bun is the answer any time of day.

Guest Check

CONTACT INFO:

758 N. Miami Ave.

CHECK NUMBER

NO 3605140

Marshall

660-886-8226

Breakfast served all day!

BREAKFAST BACK IN TIME

Marlene's Restaurant in Williamsburg is just a half mile off Interstate 70. Marlene and Joe Crane not only own a great breakfast stop, but they have other surprises here as well. Connected to the same building is the Crane's Museum. Joe has spent a lifetime collecting many kinds of antiques. Included in that facility is a banquet dining hall that serves food from Marlene's kitchen. Next door is the Crane's Country Store, which can supply your every need; or you may just want to hang out at the pot-bellied stove to chat with the locals.

Walking into the restaurant is taking a step back in time when you see eight chrome kitchen sets from the 1940s and 1950s. Their soft cushy seats are waiting for the many locals and tourists who fill the restaurant each day. If you ask the locals for the breakfast highlights, they are quick to mention Marlene's homemade sausage gravy that is usually served with the home-made biscuits. Kim Carey, who cooks each day, adds her own touch of consistency to the gravy. Each customer gets his own gravy bowl, which adds a homestyle touch that so many appreciate. The Southwest Omelets are frequently ordered for breakfast and lunch. There is no deep-frying at Marlene's.

A PERSONAL NOTE:

The secret to good, fresh gravy is using whole milk, mildly spiced sausage, and lemon pepper. Needs to be made fresh daily.

Local farmers are big contributors to Marlene's Restaurant. Taking time to stop at this special old-fashioned restaurant, museum, and country store is well worth it.

CONTACT INFO:
10665 Old Hwy. 40
Williamsburg
877-254-3356
cranesmuseum.org

LIMITED BREAKFAST HOURS

THEY CALL IT A "STRETCH"

Every day at the **Broadway Diner** in Columbia is about breakfast. This college-town diner first opened in 1949 and has a wonderful ambiance. Even though the diner was moved from Broadway to its new location to make room for a Walgreen's, the community was not about to lose their favorite breakfast stop. Ed Johnson, the owner since 1993, is proud of the diner's past and loves to tell its story.

The small, cozy establishment seating includes a counter with stools filled with hungry folks—often students. From the counter you can see lots of grilling and flipping.

The signature of this popular diner is the Stretch. It is a robust combination of three eggs, green onions, peppers, and shredded pepper jack cheese that is all grilled and served on a bed of hash browns. You can kick it up by adding chili, Tabasco sauce, and jalapeños. It's no wonder more than two hundred are served daily.

> A PERSONAL NOTE:
>
> Ed insists on fresh, thick, custom-cut bacon he gets from Patchwork Farm. He wants twelve to fifteen slices per pound, which is more than most folks offer.

The Tripleberry Pancake is another favorite. Blueberries, raspberries, and strawberries are heavily embedded in these generous-sized pancakes. New on the menu is the Breakfast Casserole. Meat, cheese, and eggs are baked into a delicious combination, and then served with fresh fruit or biscuits and gravy.

Ed believes in buying the freshest products from the local farmers, and you can tell the difference.

The popularity of this hometown landmark has other historic site information right across the street in a park-like setting. Every town should have a favorite place to call their own, just like the Broadway Diner.

"HEART DISEASE HAS CHANGED MY EATING HABITS, BUT I STILL COOK BACON FOR THE SMELL."

— George Carlin

Guest Check

CONTACT INFO:
22 S. 4th St.
Columbia
573-875-1173

CHECK NUMBER
№ 3605140

Breakfast served all day!

BREAKFAST, HISTORY, AND MYSTERY

On seven acres, right in the heart of Missouri, the town of New Franklin is the location of the **Rivercene Bed and Breakfast**. It's nestled along the bank of the Missouri River near the Katy Trail in a large mansion built by the riverboat baron Captain Joseph Kinney. The collected memorabilia of the mansion's history is on display in the grand entry hall. The elaborate home is a copy of the Governor's Mansion in Jefferson City.

The home has eleven imported fireplaces, a three-hundred-pound walnut front door, a grand staircase, and eleven bedrooms, each with its own theme. Bill and Mary Jo Alter purchased the mansion in 1994, after it had suffered a great deal of damage in the Flood of 1993.

A PERSONAL NOTE:

Just when tourist season ends, January starts the Murder Mystery events. This has been a major attraction for locals and tourists. Guests at the Rivercene are given a role to play ahead of time. You are treated to a gourmet dinner and then the fun begins.

Breakfast served in the stately dining room has an elaborate flair, just like the house. Most guests look forward to the Rivercene Cheese Soufflé. Fresh fruit and homemade pastries are great complements to the dish. Mary Jo said the simple baked omelets in individual dishes have a bottom layer of ham and a combination of cheeses before being topped with scrambled eggs that have been beaten with two hundred strokes. Dots of creamy butter are applied before baking.

This historic B&B has had much publicity through the years, including a feature story on HGTV. There are many memorable moments of good food and hospitality to take back home.

CONTACT INFO:
127 County Road 463
New Franklin
660-848-2497
rivercene.com

LIMITED BREAKFAST HOURS

TRACTORS ROLL FOR BREAKFAST

Six years ago, Karen Potter and her husband, Bill, opened the **Jackson Street Diner** in Mexico, Missouri. Their location on the town square gives it a lot of exposure, and the diner itself contains not only good food but also a collection of tractors. The Potters have been collecting tractors for many years, and when they outgrew their space at home, they brought their tractors to the diner where they could be enjoyed by all. Karen said the collection itself has become a destination.

Breakfast is big at the diner. Omelets seem to be the favorites that everyone raves about. The Philly Steak Omelet has chopped steak blended with Swiss cheese, green onions, and peppers. What about the Chicken Strip Omelet?

A PERSONAL NOTE:

Karen feels it's the vanilla she adds to the pancake mix that causes all the compliments.

Deep-fried chicken strips are united with Swiss cheese before salsa crowns the top. They are happy to make the omelets yolkless. Folks can have their say on creating their own omelet too. Yummy pancakes get many kudos, as does the Jimmy Dean Sausage and Gravy shown on the menu. Karen has been busy expanding the menu, as many breakfast diners are doing.

> "EAT BREAKFAST LIKE A KING, LUNCH LIKE A PRINCE AND DINNER LIKE A PAUPER."
>
> — Adelle Davis

Guest Check

CONTACT INFO:

SERVER | TABLE | GUESTS | CHECK NUMBER

N° 3605140

114 W. Jackson St.

Mexico

573-581-5470

Breakfast served all day!

BREAKFAST BY THE RIVER

Downtown Boonville, Missouri, aims to please the tourists as well as the locals with good food and hospitality. When you want a good breakfast, you ask the locals and they know right where to send you. Like so many towns, the best options are on Main Street, and Boonville's is called **The Riverside Diner**. Tod Bradley, with the help of his mother, Marsha, covers all the basics for breakfast.

The Riverside Slinger is quite sizable with two quarter-pound burgers and two eggs over hash browns. The heaping pile of chili on top will satisfy any appetite. If there's room, perhaps one of their eight-inch cinnamon rolls will do it for you. Omelets, French toast, and breakfast sandwiches come many ways. If you like pancakes, they won't disappoint you. Children love to order the Mickey Mouse–shaped pancakes. And no diner would be complete without their own style of biscuits and gravy.

> ## A PERSONAL NOTE:
> The restaurant believes in using ONLY purified, filtered water for all the cooking, coffee, and ice water served. They feel that quality makes the difference.

If you just want that morning or afternoon cup of coffee, the diner says they have the best coffee around. Also, all of their bakery goods are purchased fresh right down the street from the local Butternut Bakery.

The next time you drive through Boonville, slow down as you head down Main Street, because breakfast is waiting for you just steps before you cross the bridge.

> "IT'S THE COMPANY, NOT THE COOKING, THAT MAKES A MEAL."
>
> — Kirby Larson

CONTACT INFO:

201 Main St.

Boonville

660-882-6333

Breakfast served all day!

SERVER | TABLE | GUESTS | CHECK NUMBER

N⁰ 3605140

A WOODSIDE BREAKFAST

Four miles from the historic town of Hannibal is the **Garth Woodside Mansion Bed and Breakfast**. A Victorian mansion owned by Julie and John Roisen is on the thirty-nine-acre estate. They have operated this award-winning B&B since 1999. You expect amazing amenities and a wonderful breakfast with this kind of reputation, and you will find exactly that. The grounds include herbs and produce that they like to incorporate into their daily breakfasts.

A PERSONAL NOTE:

Julie says never measure what you can weigh. Pay attention to grams. It's quicker and recipes come out perfect. She also likes to keep the guests' cups on a warming plate before serving their coffee.

A guest favorite is named Eggy Cheesy to reflect the combination of eggs, five different cheeses, hash browns, corn, bacon, and red, yellow, and green peppers for the color and taste. Fresh fruit and homemade muffins are served each day. Their special blend of juice is also available, and folks would love to know their secret for what they call their Garth Juice. Breakfast is served in a glassed-in porch where you can see the beautiful setting and scenery. The room is spacious enough for small- to medium-sized groups.

John was in the Air Force for thirty-one years, so many of their recipes have been collected as they moved about the country.

The secluded mansion dominates the hilltop as you

approach the winding road to its entrance. The Dogwood House, Woodside View Cottage, and the Woodside Trail Cottage are stand-alone places to stay as well. All have themes and are modern and updated for all your needs. This Missouri bed-and-breakfast landmark continues to be rated No. 1 by the travel industry. You will likely agree, and your visit will long be remembered.

CONTACT INFO:

11069 New London Rd.

Hannibal

573-221-2789

garthmansion.com

LIMITED BREAKFAST HOURS

GYROS YOUR WAY

For a more ethnic twist on a delicious breakfast, visit **Diner 54** in Fulton. Its other location is located in Mexico, Missouri. Both are fairly new to their communities.

Jeton Alimi uses his Albanian heritage to enhance his extensive and appetizing menu. The owner and his loyal customers rave about the Gyro Skillet choice on the menu. Gyro meat, onions, and cheese are highlighted in this dish for only $6.99. There are four other skillet varieties to choose from as well, all prepared right in the skillet before baking. The skillets are then brought to you to enjoy fresh and hot. The Greek Omelet is a Grecian treat of gyro meat with feta cheese, green peppers, and tomatoes. Twelve other American omelets are tempting as well.

Crêpes make a delicious dessert, or can be a part of your breakfast menu. There are five delicious combinations to choose from.

Diner 54's décor will take you back to the fabulous 1950s. Musical instruments, vintage golf clubs, and old vinyl records are all mounted on the wall to amuse you while you eat. The nostalgic oil tablecloths are just like back in mom's kitchen.

A PERSONAL NOTE:

All of the Greek and Mediterranean meats are 70 percent lamb. They mix it with 30 percent beef, which is more pleasing to Americans.

For a breakfast that will give you an ethnic twist from your usual routine in a fun environment, give Diner 54 a visit.

> ## "HOW CAN A NATION BE GREAT IF ITS BREAD TASTES LIKE KLEENEX?"
>
> — Julia Child

CONTACT INFO:

2751 S. Clark St., Mexico

573-581-4800

2101 N. Bluff St., Fulton

573-642-7555

Breakfast served all day!

A "FOODIE" DESTINATION

Chef Tim Grandinetti is determined to make the **Clarksville Station-Overlook Farm** a food destination. Discover the Station as you explore the historic town of Clarksville, Missouri, or be a guest at one of the local bed-and-breakfasts—Rockheath House or Cedarcrest Manor. Nathalie Pettus, the Station's owner since 2004, has a very ambitious vision of the farm's success in all they offer.

Hillside gardens provide opportunities for this executive chef to prepare fresh and unique menu items. Tim's background is a culinary feast of titles, including being appointed by former Governor Matt Blunt to represent Missouri in the Food Network's Challenge series in New Orleans.

A PERSONAL NOTE:

No shortcuts on quality in this restaurant. Great products make great food. Wise choices for ingredients do make a difference.

The Station offers casual outdoor patios, café-style seating, or refined dining. Breakfast is the delight of all the B&B guests, as well as the locals and tourists. Breakfast offerings are very unusual, like the Multi-Course Nosh Tasting for a bargain of just $39.90. The tiny tasting includes three samples of pancakes with different flavored syrups; crunchy French toast bites coated in their own mix of granola; small mini quiches; tiny pecan-streusel-coffee cake; corn or walnut muffins; a small portion of their biscuits and gravy; and duck confit over flash-fried diced potatoes.

A restaurant favorite is Nathalie's Scramble. Farm fresh eggs, cream cheese, and fresh basil are served with whole-grain toast and fingerling potatoes.

Breakfast is only served on Friday, Saturday, and Sunday. It's well worth waiting for.

> **"I MYSELF PREFER MY NEW ZEALAND EGGS FOR BREAKFAST."**
>
> — Queen Elizabeth II

Guest Check

CONTACT INFO:
901 S. Hwy. 79
Clarksville
573-242-3838
overlookfarmmo.com

CHECK NUMBER
№ 3605140

Breakfast served all day!

MIX IT UP

The owners of **Café Berlin** in Columbia made friends quickly with their organic restaurant that was once a gas station. Eli Gay and Eileen McGuinn truly get the value of offering organic food in many of their menu choices. Patchwork Farms are among the ten local farmers that source their unique menu.

The Clifton "Butch" Jones for breakfast is a good example of how the café mixes it up. They take a small pancake burrito smothered with a half-order of apples and sausage. Another option to mix it up

A PERSONAL NOTE:

Regular bonuses for customers are the early bird specials plus a dollar-off coupon listed on the website.

is the John Schyler Breakfast Sandwich that stacks boiled eggs, jalapeños, bacon, red onions, tomatoes, and chipotle mayo on your choice of bread and potatoes. Vegans and vegetarians may want to try a burrito made with tempeh, which is made from forming fermented soybeans into a cake-like patty.

There are twenty-nine sides available for you to choose from to make your breakfast complete. This clever café is frequented by many students from Missouri University at Columbia. If you want a seriously good breakfast with a good cup of coffee, check out this café and "mix it up."

"My wife and I tried two or three times in the last 40 years to have breakfast together, but it was so disagreeable we had to stop."

— Winston Churchill

CONTACT INFO:

220 N. Tenth St.

Columbia

573-441-0400

cafeberlincomo.com

Breakfast served all day!

RECIPES

CRUSTLESS SPINACH QUICHE
The Southern Hotel in Ste. Genevieve, Missouri

1 cup chopped onion
1 cup sliced fresh mushrooms
1 TBSP vegetable oil
1 pkg. (10oz) frozen chopped spinach, thawed and drained
2/3 cup finely chopped, fully cooked ham
5 eggs
3 cups (12oz) shredded Monterey Jack cheese
1/8 tsp. pepper

In a large skillet, sauté onion and mushrooms in oil until tender. Add spinach and ham. Cook and stir until the excess moisture is evaporated. Cool slightly. Beat eggs, add cheese, and mix well. Stir in spinach mixture and pepper; blend well. Spread evenly into a greased 9-inch pie plate or quiche dish. Bake at 350 degrees for 40-45 minutes or until a knife inserted in the center comes out clean. Serves 6-8 people.

TWICE COOKED NEW POTATOES
The Yates House B&B in Rocheport, Missouri

12 small new Yukon or red potatoes
olive oil
sea salt and freshly grated black pepper

Scrub potatoes well. Place in saucepan and cover with water. Cook until just tender. Remove from water and place in parchment paper that has been oiled lightly to prevent sticking. Allow the potatoes to cool. Using the palm of your hand, smash each potato to break the skin and flatten slightly. Drizzle potatoes with olive oil, then sprinkle the sea salt and freshly ground pepper. Bake in pre-heated 375 degree oven until the edges are crisp and potatoes are lightly browned. It takes approximately 30 minutes. Serve hot for breakfast, lunch, or dinner.

RIVERCENE BAKED OMELET
The Rivercene B&B in Boonville, Missouri

ham slices
cheese
eggs

half and half
butter

Spray the pan with non-stick cooking spray. Line bottom of dish with slices of ham, sliced the thickness of two stacked coins. Cover with cheese slices or sprinkle grated cheese over ham to cover. I prefer Colby Jack or mozzarella, but you might prefer Swiss or cheddar. Scramble 2 eggs per person, adding half and half cream, beating 200 strokes. Pour over ham and cheese layers. Dot all with real fresh creamy butter. I use about 1 TBSP per 2 eggs.

Bake 400 degrees for 18 minutes or until done for individual dishes; 30 minutes for large baking dish. After 10 minutes in individual baking dishes or 15-20 minutes in a large dish, with a teaspoon, turn the sides in to the center so that the omelet will cook evenly. Cook until center is done. If making the large omelet, slice before serving, using fork to hold ham in place as you slice the squares. In my 11×13 baking dish, I use 12 eggs, and about ½ cup of half and half. Serving suggestions: offer Picante sauce, Tabasco sauce, Parmesan cheese.

DUTCH BABY OVEN PANCAKE
Miss Aimee B's Tea Room in St. Charles, Missouri

5 beaten eggs
1 ¼ cups milk
1 ¼ cups flour
1 tsp. vanilla

1 TBSP sugar
½ tsp. salt
1 stick unsalted butter
iron skillet

Preheat oven to 425 degrees. In a large bowl, mix eggs, milk, flour, vanilla, sugar, and salt until well blended. Heat the skillet in the oven with the 1 stick of butter for about 15 minutes. The skillet should sizzle and butter should brown. Remove from the oven and pour batter over the sizzling butter. Bake 20-25 minutes until puffed and brown. Watch to make sure the center is done. Serve warm with your choice of toppings and seasonal fruits. It serves 6-8 people.

DICKEY HOUSE BAKED HASH BROWNS
The Dickey House B&B in Marshfield, Missouri

6-8 cups fresh or frozen shredded potatoes
2 cups whole milk
4 eggs
1 cup chopped fresh green onions
½ cup chopped fresh or frozen red pepper
1 tsp. salt
dash black pepper
½ tsp. granulated garlic
2 cups shredded cheddar cheese
(optional: 6 bacon strips cooked until crisp and crumbly)

Use a greased 9×13 dish or an 8×13 metal/glass dish, buttered or sprayed with cooking spray.

Place the potatoes in a large mixing bowl. Add all ingredients one at a time, mixing between each. Mix until thoroughly moist, place in buttered dish, pressing down with a buttered spoon to compress the mixture. Bake at 375 degrees for approximately 45 minutes until the top is nicely browned and puffed. Makes 10-12 generous servings.

INDEX OF RESTAURANTS